Lernkrimi Englisch

It was MURDER, My Lord

Michael Bacon
Anne Ellsworth

Compact Verlag

Bisher sind in der Reihe Compact Lernkrimi Kurzkrimis erschienen:
- Englisch, Französisch, Italienisch, Spanisch: A2

In der Reihe Compact Lernkrimi sind erschienen:
- Englisch, Französisch, Italienisch, Spanisch: B1, B2
- Englisch GB/US, Business English: B1, B2
- Deutsch: B1
- Sammelband Lernkrimi Englisch: B1, B2

In der Reihe Compact Lernkrimi History sind erschienen:
- Englisch: B1, B2, Italienisch: B1

In der Reihe Compact Lernthriller sind erschienen:
- Englisch: B1, B2, Spanisch: B1

In der Reihe Compact Lernstory Mystery sind erschienen:
- Englisch: B1, B2

In der Reihe Compact Lernkrimi Hörbuch sind erschienen:
- Englisch: B1, B2, Business English: B2
- Französisch, Italienisch, Spanisch: B1

Lernziele:
- Grundwortschatz, Grammatik (A2, B1)
- Aufbauwortschatz, Konversation (B2)

In der Reihe Compact Schüler-Lernkrimi sind erschienen:
- Englisch, Französisch, Spanisch, Latein, Deutsch, Mathematik, Physik, Chemie

Weitere Titel sind in Vorbereitung.

Chefredaktion: Dr. Angela Sendlinger
Redaktion: Paulina Palomino
Fachredaktion: Nathalie Russell
Produktion: Wolfram Friedrich
Titelillustration: Karl Knospe
Typographischer Entwurf: Maria Seidel
Umschlaggestaltung: Carsten Abelbeck

ISBN 978-3-8174-7734-0
7277343

Besuchen Sie uns im Internet: www.compactverlag.de, www.lernkrimi.de

Vorwort

Mit den neuen, spannenden Compact Kurzkrimis können Sie Ihre Englischkenntnisse auf schnelle und einfache Weise vertiefen, auffrischen und überprüfen.

Die vier fesselnden Kurzkrimis sind ideal für geübte Anfänger und Wiedereinsteiger.

Jeder Krimi wird durch abwechslungsreiche und kurzweilige Übungen ergänzt, die das Lernen unterhaltsam und spannend machen.

Prüfen Sie Ihr Englisch in Lückentexten, Zuordnungs- und Übersetzungsaufgaben, in Buchstabenspielen und Kreuzworträtseln!

Ob im Bus oder in der Bahn, im Wartezimmer, zu Hause oder in der Mittagspause – das Sprachtraining im handlichen Format bietet die ideale Trainingsmöglichkeit für zwischendurch.

Schreiben Sie die Lösungen einfach ins Buch!

Die richtigen Antworten sind in einem eigenen Lösungsteil am Ende des Buches zusammengefasst. Im Anhang befindet sich außerdem ein Glossar, in dem die schwierigsten Wörter übersetzt sind. Diese sind im Text kursiv markiert.

Und nun kann die Spannung beginnen ...

Viel Spaß und Erfolg!

Inhalt

It Was Murder, My Lord
Bei einer Jagdveranstaltung auf dem Anwesen von Lord Bellforth wird ein Teilnehmer erschossen. Handelt es sich um einen tragischen Unfall oder kaltblütigen Mord?

Midnight in the Park
Ein amerikanisches Touristenpärchen stößt auf seiner Hochzeitsreise in London auf eine verschlüsselte Botschaft. Die beiden beginnen auf eigene Faust zu ermitteln und machen eine schreckliche Entdeckung.

Learning by Killing
Die Schüler einer Sprachschule an der Südküste Englands führen ein Kriminalstück auf. Doch aus dem Spiel wird blutiger Ernst, als das Stück tatsächlich mit einer Leiche endet.

Murder in Rosemeadows
In dem Feriendorf Rosemeadows liegt die Witwe Margaret Prim tot auf ihrem Sofa. Alles weist auf eine natürliche Todesursache hin, bis auch der Kater der Dame tot aufgefunden wird.

IT WAS MURDER, MY LORD

Michael Bacon

Chapter 1: Death

The area around Newcastle and Durham is still called Northumbria. Even today it sometimes seems to be a very wild place. You can find forests and woods, moors and small valleys with *streams* flowing into the River Wear. Not far away is Hadrian's Wall, a relic from Roman times. The Wall more or less follows what is now the border between England and Scotland.

Haddington *Manor* stands in one of these valleys, *surrounded by* woods and *ponds*. It is part of the Bellforth *estate* – a huge area just outside Durham. The English call this sort of building a "*stately home*", which is not a very accurate description. From a distance the large house looks very romantic – but when you drive up to the steps you begin to notice that Haddington *Manor* is not in a very good condition. The massive doors are rotten in places, the kitchen garden is overgrown and the window *frames* – well, it isn't the sort of house where most people would want to spend a holiday. A little villa in Tuscany or Provence offers much more than Haddington *Manor*. But when the sun shines, particularly in spring, the huge house has a certain charm. And the present owner, Lord Alfred Bellforth, plans to restore the house and the *estate* to its old glory. His wife, Harriet, and his son from his first marriage, Gordon, are working on a plan to attract *wealthy* people for weekends. What can you do in Northumbria? Well, you can ride horses, you can *pray* in Durham Cathedral, you can visit the ruins of Lindisfarne, you can look for ghosts in old *stately homes* – or you can shoot ducks with the Bellforth Shoot Company!

ÜBUNG 1 !

Übung 1: Welche Wörter gehören zusammen? Ordnen Sie zu!

1. today	[3] not precise
2. to find	[4] to finish
3. accurate ?	[5] small
4. to begin	[2] to lose
5. huge	[7] husband
6. wealthy	[1] yesterday
7. wife	[6] poor

"Mr Macey! Tell the *beaters* to start! We're all ready and waiting, here!"

"Aye, aye, my Lord. They're a good crowd. All local lads. You'll have a fine shoot this afternoon. The weather's perfect, sir!"

The sun is high in the sky. Lord Bellforth walks towards his guests and gives advice. The dogs are waiting. The silence is deafening. Then a whistle blows and all hell is let loose. The *beaters* shout and sing. The ducks come together in the middle of the *pond* and suddenly *take off*. Bang. Bang. One or two fall to the ground and then hundreds begin to fly to the north. More shots and wild cries. The dogs are busy, rushing off to *retrieve* the *booty*. And so it goes on, until around four o'clock. The shooting party finally lay down their guns and walk to a small table. Lord Bellforth points to the thermos flasks of steaming coffee and the bottles of malt whisky. He offers a toast.

"Gentlemen, my *gamekeeper*, Mr Macey, tells me that we have about 50 ducks resting over there. Not too bad; so thank you for such a good day's shooting. Those of you who are staying longer can *look forward to* several meals with duck as the main ingredient. Until then, I *suggest* we refresh ourselves with coffee – plus, of course, a glass or two!"

He raises his glass of whisky and the others all do the same. Everybody is smiling and grinning. The first day of the Bellforth Shoot Company is *obviously* a *success*.

The shooting party is relatively small. Two of them are younger, about thirty years old. They're investment bankers from the City, who are quite happy to pay £1,000 for the privilege of shooting a few ducks in the North East of England. On Sunday they'll race down the motorway back to London in their off-road 4-wheel drive cars, and in the office they'll tell their colleagues how marvellous Northumbria is and how they're thinking about buying a weekend *cottage* "up North", where they can relax for a day or two. The locals, they'll say, are all so friendly. Not particularly *bright*, but ready and willing to do a week's work for less than a bottle of champagne costs at Creevers. Creevers is the wine bar where the bankers celebrate on Friday evenings after playing around on the *Stock Exchange* and making a million or two.
There are a few relatives and family friends. Gordon, Lord Bellforth's son from his first marriage and *heir* to the *estate*, is always present at the shoots. He *runs* a public relations company in London. In fact, it's his idea to organize the shooting parties for his father. In this day and age, he says, you must *preserve* the past by *exploiting* the present. He's already thinking about how he can describe the present scene in an advertising brochure. "Sun, good company, faithful dogs, plenty of ducks, woods, an old *manor* house, etc. etc." His good friend, David Barrington-Jones, is also present. It's his first visit to the Bellforth *estate*. He and Gordon went to the same school, Gosling College, one of the best independent schools in Britain. David comes from a well-established family in Cheshire. He's the managing director of Tingworth, a traditional firm that specializes in English *pottery*. Some people say

that he's worth at least £200 million. Like Gordon, he is aged 35, unmarried, and simply having fun. Life has so much to offer!

ÜBUNG 2 !

Übung 2: Welches Wort ist das „schwarze Schaf"? Unterstreichen Sie das nicht in die Reihe passende Wort!

1. awful, fine, marvellous, perfect
2. table, coffee, whisky, water
3. duck, dog, gamekeeper, horse
4. day, afternoon, motorway, week
5. family, stranger, friend, relative
6. pond, wood, valley, wine bar
7. organize, weekend, specialize, fly

As the shooting party chatter and drink coffee and whisky, George Macey, the *gamekeeper* and the real Master of Ceremonies, orders the local men to put the *booty* in a Landrover and deliver it to the kitchens.

"Jim, Jim Hardcastle! Be careful with those ducks. The gentlemen will have the breasts, but there's a good soup left in all of them. And that's for us, you know!"

Jim Hardcastle, the head *beater*, a middle-aged *fellow* from the local village, turns to Macey.

"Aye," he says. "The gentlemen always get the breasts. Nothing wrong with that, Mr Macey."

He grins and makes a rather obscene gesture. The *gamekeeper* laughs and *pretends* to *cuff* Hardcastle *round the ear*. He likes his head *beater*. They work well together, and if Gordon's plans are *successful*, there'll be plenty of work in the future. There's very little industry in the area nowadays and unemployment is high. For a moment, Macey *vividly* remembers his childhood. Coalmining and shipbuilding! Regular work and good pay! A hard life but one full of rewards. Yes, the good old days with *brass bands* and working-men's clubs. It may, just may all happen again – if Gordon can attract enough of these young bankers. My God, thinks Macey, they've got money to throw around.

As the shooting party move off to their transport, a transit-van suddenly *pulls up*. This is Harriet, the wife of Lord Bellforth. A very attractive woman, aged 42, and much younger than her husband, who is already over 60. She jumps out, rushes towards her husband and kisses him on both cheeks.

"Alfred," she exclaims. "How was it? A good shoot? How many? I have to organize everything with the kitchen *staff*."

Lord Bellforth gives his wife the details and then turns to the other members of the party. Gordon walks up to Harriet, David by his side.

"Harriet, a marvellous shoot! We've got around 50 nice, fat ducks! I hope the freezers are working! But let me introduce David – you know, my old friend from schooldays."

Harriet and David shake hands.

"Now it's all up to you, Harriet. But you'll *manage*, I know. By the way, make sure you look after those two over there." Gordon points to the investment bankers. "They're multipliers. If they go back to London happy, then we can expect at least another ten at the next shoot. They know nothing about guns but they've got money, real money!"

Gordon, the son and *heir* of Lord Bellforth, the man who wants to *preserve* his *inheritance*, rushes off to make sure that the *booty* is transported safely. David is left standing with Harriet. There's a pause in the conversation, whilst Harriet wonders how to *cope with* about 50 dead ducks.

"So, you're David? David from the *pottery* clan! Pleased to meet you. Gordon is always talking about you."

! ÜBUNG 3

Übung 3: Lesen Sie weiter und unterstreichen Sie alle elf Pronomen im folgenden Textabschnitt!

David Barrington-Jones stands astonished in front of Harriet. He sees a remarkably attractive woman, about the same height. She has dark hair, brown eyes, a slim *figure* and a healthy *complexion*.
"Yes, Lady Bellforth. That's right, Gordon and I were at school together. We often meet up in London. We're both members of the same club."
"Oh, David. Forget the Lady Bellforth thing. Call me Harriet – everybody else in Haddington does. Come on, why don't we give the servants a hand with some of these plates and *napkins*?"
Harriet and David help to load up the table and all the rest into the van. Harriet is quite *impressed* by Gordon's friend. He has short, black hair and is very *handsome*. She hopes he can visit them more often.

Then Lord Bellforth marches back. He grins broadly and claps his hands in delight.
"Well, my dear, this shoot can pay for the kitchen garden. Wonderful day! And this is just the beginning! Now, Gordon and I are going back with Macey. The others have all got their own transport. Can you *give* David *a lift*? Otherwise there isn't enough room."
Harriet opens the door of the transit van and flashes a smile.
"OK, hop in David. Let's see whether we can get back to the house before the others."
Various vehicles begin to *rev up*. And then there's a wild chase

through the valleys and moors. The bankers are ecstatic. Harriet is a good driver but David feels a little nervous. Who cares? It's like a go-kart race and it's all off-road. As Lord Bellforth, Gordon and Macey arrive at the *Manor*, Harriet and David *pull up*. The bankers, of course, are the winners. Aren't they always?

Later in the evening, inside the *manor* house, the guests are sitting around the large dining table. The meal is magnificent. Harriet certainly knows how to organize the kitchen *staff* and all the cooking. The two bankers are enjoying a bottle of port and smoking their cigars. The older one, Toby Seaton, is trying to persuade David Barrington-Jones to invest a large sum of money in a *wind farm* that his company is financing. His friend seems much more interested in Sally Hardcastle, the head *beater's* wife, who has a part-time job serving the weekend guests. Lord Bellforth is sitting in front of a large fire, *sipping* his whisky, when Harriet returns from the kitchen.
"Well, my lord and master?" she enquires, dropping into an armchair. "Everything OK?"
"It couldn't be better, Harriet. Gordon's idea for the Bellforth Shoot Company is a marvellous *success*. The dinner was excellent. And now, my dear, I think, at least for me, it's time to get a good night's sleep."
And so Lord Bellforth, tired but happy, takes his leave from the others and disappears upstairs.

Übung 4: Welche Wörter gehören zusammen? Ordnen Sie zu!

ÜBUNG 4 !

1. to go back	[7] around a table
2. to give	[5] in a person

3. to flash	☐ at the house
4. to arrive	☐ a cigar
5. to be interested	☐ with someone
6. to sip	☐ a smile
7. to sit	☐ someone a lift
8. to smoke	☐ money
9. to invest	☐ a drink

A few months later, another shooting party is *gathered* under the trees. The investment bankers are there again, this time with about fifteen colleagues. Gordon is pleased. He knows he can now make enough money to repair the *outhouses* and have something left over! David, who is now a regular visitor to Haddington, is a member of the party again. However, Alfred Bellforth feels slightly uncomfortable. Yes, the money's coming in, thanks to Gordon. But things are different! He doesn't know exactly what, but he has a feeling that something is not quite right. During the après-shoot dinner, Bellforth drinks a little too much wine and decides to leave early. Lying in bed, he thinks again about the changes over the last few months. Are there really any problems? Well, to be honest, there are. For a start those bankers! Awful people! They have no relationship to the countryside. They enjoy a good day's shooting; they enjoy the results – roast duck and the occasional piece of *venison*. Then they bring in whole boxes of wine, champagne and whisky. And the way they behave! They don't dress for dinner, they light cigars with £20 *notes*, they talk shop and can't even hold a knife and fork properly! Lord Bellforth often leaves the dinner table at an early hour and goes to bed. He's fond of Gordon, but wonders whether this is really the right way to keep the *estate* in the family. And then there's that friend of Gordon's – David Barrington-Jones! Why is he always here, almost a permanent guest nowadays? Something, somewhere, somehow, is not quite right, thinks Lord Bellforth. And then he turns over and settles into a restless sleep.

The next day, Mr Macey gives the signal, as usual. The guns fire and the ducks fall. The dogs sit and wait. They want to do their job. Everything is going smoothly until the party hear a shout from the back. It's Toby Seaton, one of the bankers.
"Here, help! Man down! Wounded! Fetch a doctor, quickly. Oh my God! He's dying!"
For about thirty seconds there is total silence, and then everybody runs to the scene. Some of them *grab* their mobiles. The shooting party assembles around the body of the dead man. Nothing can be done. David Barrington-Jones is lying in the grass, blood trickling out of his mouth and a *gaping* gunshot wound under his shoulder.

Übung 5: Enträtseln Sie die folgenden Definitionen!

ÜBUNG 5 !

1. A person who works with money: banker (rkebna)

2. A person who belongs to a club or a party:

member (rbeemm)

3. You use it to eat: fork (kofr)

4. A person you like: friend (dnrefi)

5. A loud cry: shout (tsuho)

6. A telephone: mobile (eblimo)

7. A part of the body: shoulder (rdeluhos)

Chapter 2: Questions

Inspector Davidson from Newcastle is sitting in the local police station of Haddington. A Northerner through and through, he feels uncomfortable with the young, well-dressed Londoner before him.

"So, your name is Seaton, Toby Seaton. And what do you do for a living, sir?"

"I'm an investment banker, Inspector. I invest money and make money. For my clients, for the bank and, *in the final analysis*, for myself."

Davidson *shifts around* in his chair. He doesn't like the la-di-da accent of Toby Seaton. He doesn't like the fact that Toby Seaton probably earns more in a week than he earns in a year. In fact, he doesn't even like the name Toby. Inspector Davidson takes out a cigarette, lights it and looks out the window.

"Now, Toby – may I call you Toby?"

Seaton *nods*. He's not quite sure whether Inspector Davidson is being *polite* or sarcastic.

"OK, Toby – there you are, at the back of the party. Lord Bellforth is shooting his mouth off – excuse me – giving instructions about how to raise the gun at the right time and all that. Are you following me, Toby?"

Seaton *nods* again. He wants to get back to the City. This whole affair has nothing to do with him. Creevers, the wine bar in London, is much more pleasant than a police station in the North East of England. But then he remembers something.

"No, one moment, Inspector. Lord Bellforth isn't there. It's just me and David."

Inspector Davidson makes a *note* and continues.

"And then, when the guns all *go off*, Barrington-Jones, the *fellow* next to you, falls down. Is that right?"

Seaton shudders in his chair.
"Look, Inspector. I have a very important deal tomorrow. There is a lot of money *involved*. You've got my *statement*. I know nothing more than you. Barrington-Jones is standing next to me and I'm giving him the latest news about this *wind farm* project – that's the deal tomorrow. A few months earlier, when I met him for the first time, he was very interested. And he's got a lot of cash to invest. Now he's not so sure. His *circumstances*, he says, are different. Well, you can imagine my feelings! We're talking about at least five million here. 'OK, David,' I say. 'Let's go through the details again this evening.' Then the ducks begin to fly up and a few minutes later Barrington-Jones is on the ground, bleeding from the mouth. I really can't help you further."
Davidson grunts. He seems to be getting nowhere.
"OK, Toby. We've already got your written *statement*. If there are any further questions, I can contact you by phone, can't I?"
Toby Seaton stands up and takes a card from his wallet.
"Certainly, Inspector. But use this number – it's my private line. The other one is for business. Sorry I can't be of more help. And believe me, Barrington-Jones is the last person I want to see dead. But I suppose it's too late now. I've got no signed papers for the deal. The whole thing's a disaster."
Davidson makes a few *notes* as Toby Seaton leaves the office. He's not totally convinced that the banker is telling the truth – but then how many bankers do tell the truth? In his experience, none. There's a knock at the door and the local policeman, Sergeant Emsley, enters.
"Sir, it's Lord Bellforth. He says it's *urgent*. Shall I show him in?"
The inspector looks unhappy. He doesn't actually dislike His Lordship, but on the other hand, the man is rather a *pain in the neck*. Old-fashioned, pompous and, to be honest, a bit of a snob. He

knows Bellforth from a couple of *investigations* concerning *poaching* – and the *poacher* is still out there, somewhere in the wilds of Northumbria. In fact, one of the *suspects* comes from the Hardcastle family. It's one of those *cases* which are still open but, as far as Davidson is concerned, temporarily closed. Alfred Bellforth marches into the office and sits down immediately. He appears to be very *worried*.

ÜBUNG 6

Übung 6: Bringen Sie die Wörter in die richtige Reihenfolge!

1. uncomfortable young he the feels Londoner with

2. shifts chair inspector around his in the

3. do nothing him affair has with the to

4. statement we got already written your have

5. rather neck Bellforth in is the pain a

6. door there at is the a knock

7. appears worried he very be to

"Good of you to see me, Inspector. I've got some important news. The gun that Barrington-Jones used. You've got it here, haven't you? Well, it seems that it's *faulty* – likely to *backfire*, says my gun *steward*. It should be at Barker's, the *gunsmith's*, for repair, but somehow, on the day of the shoot, it ended up in Barrington-Jones's hands. I can't understand why! This is all most unfortunate. For God's sake, don't say anything to the press yet. This whole affair might ruin me!"

Davidson stands up and lights another cigarette. "Are you telling me, Lord Bellforth, that all of this was just an accident?"

"Of course it was! Crystal clear, isn't it? We *issue* the guns just before the shoot begins and collect them immediately after. This particular gun – here's the registration number: A5023 – is unsafe according to a report from last week's shoot. The *cartridges* jam in the *barrels* and so there's a possibility that it may *backfire*. That must be the explanation. The gun at Barker's has the number A5033. It seems to be a *case* of human *error*. You'll want to interview my *gamekeeper* Mr Macey, of course. And Taylor, he's the gun *steward*. But, in their defence, let me say now that the fault cannot possibly lie with them."

The inspector makes a few more *notes*. He knows very well that the Bellforth Shoot Company provides employment for the local people. With a bit of luck he can close the *case* quickly. After all, accidents do happen. Bellforth is still talking about the organization of the weekend shoots.

Übung 7: Lesen Sie weiter und setzen Sie die richtige Verbform ein!

"...and so you see, Inspector, on the one hand they (1. bring) ____________________ in a fair amount of money, which (2. go)

ÜBUNG 7 !

__________ towards the upkeep of the house and (3. give) __________ so many locals a regular job or a bit of extra cash. You know, we employ about twenty young men to do the beating. And then there (4. be) __________ the kitchen *staff*. The customers – or the 'punters', as my son Gordon (5. call) __________ them – (6. be) __________ mostly these young bankers from down South. I can't say I (7. like) __________ them. They have no manners, no style, think they can poke their noses into this or that room. Their knowledge of country life is absolutely zero. But they (8. have) __________ the money and the money (9. end) __________ up here in Haddington."

Inspector Davidson leans back in his chair and looks up quickly. Bellforth, he thinks, is trying to *convince* me that this death is simply an accident. Why? He remembers that Alfred Bellforth is married to a very attractive woman who is much younger than her husband. Maybe Barrington-Jones and Lady Bellforth are connected in some way? It's quite possible that an old man could decide to commit murder to save his marriage. Doesn't every aristocratic family have at least one *skeleton in the cupboard*? Davidson focuses once more on Lord Bellforth, who is now beginning to *sweat*.

"...and when the guns are *issued*, these bankers all *fuss around*, laughing and cackling. They seem to think that a duck-shoot is some sort of game, like Cowboys and Indians. No wonder things often get *muddled up*. But we're covered by insurance, you know. Everyone has to sign a contract saying that they accept full *responsibility* for anything that goes wrong."

Lord Bellforth stands up to shake hands with Davidson.

"So, old man, that's all cleared up. Shame for Barrington-Jones – and his family, of course. But when you play with fire, you must expect accidents to happen."

And with these final words, Lord Bellforth leaves the police station and gets into his Bentley. Inspector Davidson watches him from the window. He's not sure about Bellforth and he's not sure about Seaton. And Harriet Bellforth? Also a question mark. Davidson, the son of a coalminer, wonders whether he's prejudiced. But he's only too happy to *shelve the case*, if possible. There are other, more serious problems concerning murder and *rape* in nearby Newcastle. Let's have a word with George Macey, the *gamekeeper*. Perhaps he can throw some light on the *case*? He goes to the door.

"Emsley? Is George Macey still there?"

"Yes, sir. Shall I brew up a pot of tea?"

The *gamekeeper* walks into the office. He knows Davidson from the *poaching case*. They both come from the same sort of working class background. The sergeant brings in the tea. Davidson begins.

"George, good to see you again. Why don't you tell me your version of the events."

Macey drinks his tea in silence for a few moments.

"Look, Jack, I can only tell you what I know. There's a fairly large party for the shoot at the weekend. His Lordship *fusses around* as usual and then goes back to the *Manor*, leaving me *in charge*. Then it happens – with Barrington-Jones. I call the ambulance immediately, but the *fellow* is clearly dead. When I go back to report, I see Bellforth in the gun-room. He's shouting at poor old Taylor and saying something about a possible *mix-up*. Joe Taylor is checking gun tickets. He's running around looking at numbers, comparing them with Barker's, the gun-smith's. I tell His Lordship that the *bloke,* Barrington-Jones, is dead. And then Bellforth storms off. That's all I know, Jack."

Inspector Davidson picks up his *notes*.

"OK, George. I'm going to leave it there. In my opinion, it seems to be an accident. Now it's up to the *coroner's court* – and, of course, the insurance companies. Nothing to do with the police anymore."

Davidson and Macey stand up, shake hands and say goodbye to Sergeant Emsley. Davidson drives off to Newcastle, a long day now over. Macey heads back to his *cottage*.

ÜBUNG 8!

Übung 8: Welche der folgenden Aussagen sind wahr? Markieren Sie mit richtig ✔ oder falsch – !

1. Bellforth knows why David had the wrong gun. ☐
2. People get the guns just before the shoot begins. ☐
3. The registration number of the faulty gun is A5023. ☐
4. Many local people work for the Bellforth Shoot Company. ☐
5. Bellforth is a "punter". ☐
6. Inspector Davidson's father was a policeman. ☐
7. Davidson and Macey know each other. ☐

Harriet is sitting in the main lounge when Bellforth returns.

Poor David, she thinks. She just can't understand how something like this could happen. Look to the future, she thinks. It was only an accident. Life goes on. When her husband enters the room and pours himself a strong whisky, she begins to cry.

Bellforth turns round sharply.

"You can cut that out, Harriet. Wrong time, wrong place!"
He walks to the fireplace and stands facing her.
"It was an accident, Harriet. Even that bloody Inspector Davidson *agrees*. There's nothing more that can be done. Every man has to check his own gun, dammit. Why are you so *upset*?"
Harriet wipes away her tears.
"Of course, Alfred. I'm being silly and stupid. It's just that David, he's such a pleasant young man. It's just not fair. I mean..."
"WAS, Harriet. Barrington-Jones WAS such a pleasant young man, as you put it. He's dead now. And there's an end to it."
The atmosphere becomes icy. Neither Lord Bellforth nor his wife really wants to continue the conversation. Nobody likes talking about death. They *stare* at each other for several long seconds. Then Bellforth storms out of the room as Harriet starts crying again.

Three weeks later the *inquest* into the death of David Barrington-Jones takes place. Bellforth and his wife are present. Gordon is sitting next to them. Several of the people in the shooting party of that fateful day are also in the court, amongst them Mr Macey, Mr Taylor, the gun *steward*, and a representative from Barker's, the *gunsmith's*. A *lawyer* from Chester, who represents the interests of Tingworth *Pottery*, is also there, as well as representatives from various other insurance companies. Lord Bellforth *feels ill at ease*. After all, the future of the Bellforth shooting parties – and thus the future of the Bellforth *estate* – hangs on the *outcome*. His *blood pressure* is high and he constantly *fidgets* in his chair. In fact, he behaves just like someone who has a bad *conscience*. Harriet also looks uncomfortable but sits quietly in her seat. All the *evidence* is presented and then the coroner *adjourns* for lunch. Gordon takes his father and step-mother to the pub nearby.

ÜBUNG 9 !

Übung 9: Lesen Sie weiter und setzen Sie die Verben im folgenden Textabschnitt in die Present Simple Form!

"Father, you must *calm down*. There's no need to worry. Accidents (1. happen) ________________. Unfortunately, in this *case*, to one of my old school friends. But we (2. be) ________________ covered by the insurance, and remember, all the members of a shooting party (3. sign) ________________ a contract. We, the Bellforth Shoot Company, (4. accept) ________________ no *responsibility* for accidents. Every man (5. have) ________________ to check the gun he (6. get) ________________."

Alfred Bellforth (7. take) ________________ another sip of whisky. "Yes, yes, my boy," he *sighs*. "But what happens if they say that it isn't an accident. An accident (8. be) ________________ bad enough – but perhaps it's murder. Who knows?"

Harriet turns as *white as a sheet* and reaches for the table *napkin*. She's sure that her husband *suspects* her of having an affair with Barrington-Jones. But why is he now talking about murder? Gordon *brushes* the comment *aside*.

"Please don't be absurd, father. David was one of the most decent people I know. In business matters as well as in private matters. This isn't a *case* of murder. We're talking about an accident, a tragic accident. A *mix-up* with the guns. We all know that those bankers are a bit wild. It's Taylor that I feel sorry for. He probably thinks that everything is his fault."

Lord Bellforth *sighs* and *nods* his head. He seems to be ten years older than he really is.

"Yes, poor Taylor. He's absolutely sure that there was no mistake. But then how does gun A5023, the *faulty* gun, end up in David's hands. I just can't understand it!"

"Neither can I," says Gordon. "But let's hope for the best. And the business is not affected in the slightest. All the shoots are booked up till Christmas."

They eat their meal in silence. None of them feels particularly hungry, so they order another few drinks and return to the court. The coroner *sums up* all the facts and then stands up. He *pronounces his judgment* in one brief sentence. The Bellforths *heave a sigh of relief*. The *inquest* decides that David Barrington-Jones's death is the result of an unfortunate accident. Nobody is to blame.

Chapter 3: Developments

Two years later, George Macey is watching the news on TV whilst Mrs Macey is washing up the dishes in the kitchen. Things in Haddington are looking up. Old Lord Bellforth is *taking a back seat* and Gordon is organizing more and more shoots, even bringing in foreigners. The Bellforth Shoot Company is expanding and the local farmers are also opening up their land. The *Manor* House is now totally *refurbished* and there is even a plan to turn it into a hotel, open all year. Harriet is organizing that side of the business and, in Macey's opinion, doing a very good job. In fact, the whole idea of catering for *wealthy* customers is a *success*. You have to change with the times, thinks Macey. Old habits die hard – but the *Manor* House is now standing in all its former glory, the dogs are still there, more than ever before, the woods and *ponds* are all in perfect order. He remembers a slogan from the local Member of Parliament: "In order to keep tradition we need change". How true, thinks Macey, how very true! On the TV screen they're showing this year's *Trooping the Colour*. The Queen is taking the Royal Salute. As the various Regiments march past, the military bands switch from one melody to another. But then something seems to be wrong. There's an irritating little *jingle* that becomes louder and louder. Suddenly Macey realizes that his mobile is ringing.

"Yes," he *growls*. "Who is it? Can I ring you back?"

The voice at the other end seems *familiar* but he can't quite place it.

"Mr Macey, sorry to disturb you but we've got a bit of an accident."

"Who is this? What's the problem? Something to do with the shoot next weekend?" Macey is now very *alert*.

"It's John Fisk speaking, sir. And it's about Jim Hardcastle, the *bloke in charge* of us *beaters*. He's dead, Mr Macey. Driving back from the pub. His car went off the road – you know, the sharp *bend* on Blackthorn Lane with all those trees. The police and the ambulance are here but there's nothing we can do. Can you come down – I'm not quite sure how this may affect arrangements for the shoot."

Damnation, thinks Macey and turns off the TV. He rushes out to the hall, puts on his shoes and coat and then calls to his wife in the kitchen.

"Dolly, something's come up. *Urgent*! Hardcastle, the head *beater*. Dead, it seems. I'll be back as soon as possible."

And with that Macey rushes out and heads towards the scene of the accident.

Mrs Macey dries the last plate. Oh dear, she thinks. This means trouble. Still, George will sort everything out. And in the meantime she can switch over to BBC1 and watch the film with that charming young man called Hugh Brant – or whatever his name is.

Übung 10: Welche Wörter haben eine ähnliche Bedeutung? Ordnen Sie zu!

ÜBUNG 10 !

1. to calm down	☐ trouble
2. napkin	☐ important
3. to brush aside	☐ to relax
4. to understand	☐ street
5. melody	☐ plans
6. arrangements	☐ to ignore
7. urgent	☐ to comprehend
8. road	☐ serviette
9. problem	☐ tune

Ten minutes later Macey is at the scene of the accident – one police car, one ambulance and John Fisk. Standing by the police car is Inspector Davidson. Macey remembers him from the *inquest* and the *poaching incident* a couple of years ago. Pleasant *chap*, much more interested in serious crime in Newcastle than accidents in Haddington. Macey gets out of his car and sees the wreck of a Ford. The car is totally destroyed.

"Evening, George. Jack Davidson. We..."

"Of course, Inspector. That unfortunate thing with the *chap* from the *pottery* company. But what are you doing here?"

"Pure *coincidence*, pure *coincidence*! I'm still looking for that *poacher*, you know. Sergeant Emsley is driving me back to the station when we get a call about a traffic accident. That's why we're here. Awful thing. But you know the poor *chap*, so Fisk tells me?"

"Yes, yes, of course I know him. You're talking about Jim Hardcastle, our head *beater*. A very *reliable fellow*. Oh dear, this creates problems for next weekend. Sorry, Jack, I'm thinking about business now. Please forgive me."

While the police and the ambulance talk about details, Macey turns to John Fisk.

"Well done John! Thanks for calling me. You must take over poor Jim's job for the time being. There's a lot of money *at stake* for the next shoot."

Fisk is rather *embarrassed* and shakes his head.

"I'm not sure about that Mr Macey. There are things you need to know – and perhaps His Lordship doesn't want to know. And the police, well..."

The two men move off the road as the ambulance switches on its siren and takes the body away. Davidson and Emsley wave and then follow the ambulance in the police car.

"Well, come on, John. Out with it! What do you want to tell me?"

Macey is *impatient*. He can see that he must reorganize things for the next shoot, which is only two days away.

"Why can't you take over as head *beater*? My God, you *know the ropes* well enough!"

John Fisk *frowns* and then turns to Macey.

"Mr Macey, I'm still a bit shaken. Let's head back to your place and then I can tell you what's troubling me."

Shortly after ten in the evening the two men arrive back at the *gamekeeper's cottage*. Dolly is in the living-room watching the film, so Macey decides to use the kitchen. Fisk sits down. He seems more *composed* now. Macey brews a pot of tea and takes a chair.

"Milk and sugar, John?"

"Aye, thanks. Two spoons, please."

"Now, let's hear what you have to tell me. My wife won't disturb us, so it's between you and me."

Fisk *sips* his tea and begins to recount the events of the evening.

Übung 11: Setzen Sie die Verben in die richtige Form (Present Simple oder Present Progressive)!

"There I am in the pub. I (1. play) ______________ a game of darts with a friend of mine, when Jim Hardcastle (2. walk) ______________ in. He looks a little *worse for wear* – you (3. know) ______________, four or five pints of beer under his belt and a bit too friendly. He (4. see) ______________ me and calls me over, orders a pint and asks me what I (5. have) ______________. I say no thanks – what with the car and so on. I can't *afford* to lose my driving licence. Then he (6. give) ______________ a *loopy* grin and says that his wife (7. leave) ______________ him."

Macey interrupts.
"You mean Sally – Sally Hardcastle? That's a shame. She's a *grand* woman, and those two boys – what are their names again, Peter and... the other one?"
"Rodney," says Fisk. "Yeah, they're two fine young lads. I'm as surprised as you are, Mr Macey. So I ask him why, and he comes out with this story. Well, I don't know whether to believe it or not!"
"Go on," says Macey in an *encouraging* tone.
"Jim says that his wife, Sally, keeps telling him to go to the police and make a *statement* – a *statement* about that accident a couple of years ago with the *bloke* from the *pottery* firm – what was his name again?"
"Barrington-Jones," replies Macey. "Yes, that awful accident with the *faulty* gun."

"But that's exactly the point, Mr Macey. According to Jim it isn't an accident. It's *deliberate*. Now remember, Jim is fairly drunk at this point. But he says that he saw His Lordship go up to the poor *chap* and *exchange* guns soon after the party arrived behind the woods. And then Lord Bellforth marches off back to the *Manor* House and half-an-hour later, when the ducks fly up, the punters begin to shoot and suddenly that *bloke*, Barrington-Jones, is down on the ground. And... well you remember the rest, of course."

Macey *nods* slowly and begins to *put two and two together*. He thinks back. Yes, it's quite true. When that investment banker shouted out, Lord Bellforth was no longer with the party. And when they finally returned to the *Manor* House, Bellforth was in the gun-room talking to Taylor in that loud, aggressive voice he has, in fact more or less *accusing* Taylor of making a mistake. And then the *inquest*! Bellforth sitting in the courtroom, *sweating* and *fidgeting* in his chair. Can it be that his employer, Alfred Bellforth, is a murderer? Macey wants to find out more.

"Come on, John. Any other information?"

"Sorry, Mr Macey, that's all I know. Jim Hardcastle is on his third pint and then suddenly decides to leave. Must find Sally, he says, she can't leave me like this. And then he rushes out to the car and drives off. I try to stop him but it's too late, so I follow in my own car. And then the stupid fool takes that corner too fast – he must be doing about 80 miles per hour – and crashes straight into the tree. There's no way I can help poor old Jim, so I call the *emergency* services and a little later the ambulance arrives, along with the *coppers*."

The *gamekeeper* finishes his tea. All of this is very unsettling and the next shoot is *looming on the horizon*. He clears up the cups and leads Fisk to the door.

"OK, John. Leave this with me. Say nothing to anyone about your conversation with Jim Hardcastle. I can contact you after I find out

more. But, until then, you must remain silent. And – you must take over the *beaters* for Saturday. There's more than 20,000 *quid at stake*. As well as your job, my job and the jobs of all the other men. OK? Do you want a minicab or can you drive back to your place?"
"No, Mr Macey. I can drive. And you can *rely on* me. Not a word about my conversation with Jim."
"And the *beaters* on Saturday?" asks Macey. It's difficult to decide whether the *gamekeeper* is more interested in *solving* a possible murder *case* or in making sure that the shoot can take place.
"OK, Mr Macey," says Fisk. "I suppose I can *manage* it. As of now I'm your new head *beater*."

Before he goes to bed, Macey opens the door of the living room. The film is almost finished. Several people are driving around London in a car and trying to avoid the *traffic jams*. Dolly is fast asleep on the sofa, snoring gently. He taps her on the shoulder once, twice. No response. All well and good, he thinks to himself. I must get a good night's sleep. I may be a *gamekeeper*, but tomorrow I must do a swift bit of detective work.

Übung 12: Übersetzen Sie folgende Sätze ins Deutsche!

ÜBUNG 12 !

1. He must make a statement to the police.

____

2. You remember the rest, of course.

____

3. Bellforth is talking in an aggressive voice.

____

4. Fisk has got some information.

5. Suddenly he decides to leave.

6. You can rely on me totally.

7. He opens the door to the living room.

Chapter 4: Peace

At eight o'clock the next morning the *gamekeeper* is standing in the office of Haddington *Manor*. Macey tells Harriet about the accident and says that he must speak to Lord Bellforth immediately. They need a new head *beater* and he wants to *suggest* John Fisk for the position. After about twenty minutes Bellforth *shuffles* in and *slumps* into his chair.

"Morning, Mr Macey. This is awful news. Quite awful! Hardcastle was a good man. But we can talk about that later. Let's get down to business."

Like Macey, Bellforth realizes that they need a *replacement*. You can't have a *successful* shoot if the *beaters* don't get the right orders at exactly the right moment.

"Harriet tells me you want to put in John Fisk. I can't put a face to the name. Is he any good?"

"Well, my Lord, he hasn't got the experience of Jim Hardcastle.

He's a little younger. But I'm pretty sure he can do the job. It's a big shoot and we really have no alternative."

Bellforth *nods*. He seems rather *drowsy*, probably the result of too much whisky the night before, thinks Macey.

"Poor old Jim," he says. "What a way to go. Too much of the local ale, I suppose. Just like his father – heavy drinkers, the Hardcastles. Right, Mr Macey, tell Fisk that he can have the position of head *beater*. You can sort out the details about pay and bonuses with Gordon. He's arriving this afternoon."

And with that Lord Bellforth gets out of his chair with much more energy than before. He seems to be almost glad that Jim Hardcastle is dead. Walking to the window, he looks out over the *estate*. Blue skies, no *clouds*. A shame about Jim, but accidents do happen. He turns to Macey and smiles.

"You know, George, this is all very tragic, but *every cloud has a silver lining*. I think this weekend's shoot will be a great *success*. We've got twenty guns, all paying £1,000 a head! Some of them from the Continent, thanks to Gordon! The weather's good. Harriet has everything under control. You have the *beaters*, the ducks, the dogs and so on. My God, George, I feel twenty years younger!"

Macey takes his leave. It's rare for Lord Bellforth to address him by his first name. For some reason His Lordship is very happy. Has he really got a *skeleton in the cupboard*?

George Macey is in his car. He rings through to John Fisk, tells him that he's got the job and then gives details about the shoot and the *beaters*. Now he must stop by at Jim Hardcastle's place and find out more about "the *statement*". As he *pulls up*, Sally Hardcastle is loading a van with pieces of furniture. Her two sons are standing next to the front door.

"Hello, Sally," says Macey. He *nods* to the two boys. "I'm so terribly sorry about Jim. Can I help in any way? The kids? They can stay with us until the *funeral* is over and done with. It's your choice, of course."

Sally Hardcastle *stares* at Macey for a few seconds. She's holding a small framed photo, and then she suddenly throws it into the garden. She begins to cry. Macey holds her tight and signals to the boys. Go inside, he's saying. Go inside. Peter and Rodney run into the *cottage*.

"Sally, Sally! *Calm down*. This isn't the end of the world! Life goes on! Come on, love. Let's go and have a cup of tea and talk things over."

In the kitchen they sit down. Macey is pretty miserable. After all, Sally's husband is dead. The two boys have no father. He wants to do his best and yet he knows that the information he has from John Fisk may be the *death-blow* for Haddington *Manor*. Lord Bellforth, the murderer of David Barrington-Jones? The whole business could *fold up*. Jobs, including his own, could disappear.

"Now listen to me, Sally. I want the truth. John Fisk tells me that your decision to leave Jim has something to do with the Barrington-Jones accident – you remember, two years ago. Something to do with making a *statement* to the police."

Sally Hardcastle bursts into tears again. Macey offers her a *handkerchief*, which she accepts. She dries her eyes.

"George, you're a good man. Jim always said that. But you don't know the half of it. It's me who is to blame! Me!"

Macey starts thinking, very fast. What does Sally Hardcastle mean? How is she to blame? Rodney appears round the door.

"Mum," he says, very quietly. "Mum, what about my *stamp* collection? Can I keep it, or shall I throw it away?"

Sally Hardcastle stands up and talks to her son in a whisper. She returns to the table. Macey has a very distinct feeling that *clouds never have silver linings*, and this *cloud* is becoming ever darker.

“Right, Sally. Now you must be honest with me! Something is very wrong here, and I must know what it is!”

The sun is shining through the kitchen window, sparkling on the cups and saucers. Sally Hardcastle, thirty-five years old, a mother of two and now a *widow*, a very attractive woman, begins to *reveal* everything. A beautiful, glorious day for a terrible *confession*.

“Yes, George. You’re right. You must know everything. Here’s the story.”

Sally Hardcastle sits rigidly in her chair and begins.

Übung 13: Beantworten Sie folgende Fragen auf Englisch!

ÜBUNG 13 !

1. Where is Macey at eight o’clock the next morning?

____

2. What do you need for a successful shoot?

____

3. When is Gordon arriving?

____

4. Where do Macey and Sally sit down and talk?

____

5. What does Macey give Sally when she begins to cry?

____

6. What does Rodney not want to throw away?

7. What is the weather like when Macey visits Sally Hardcastle?

"That summer, two and a half years ago, I can remember the day exactly. One of the first shoots. I'm serving the supper in the evening. You know that I help out on the weekends. Lord Bellforth is at the top of the table, chatting with Harriet and the guests. Everything's a great *success*. Money coming in. Fantastic prospects. All thanks to Gordon, who wants to keep Haddington *Manor* and expand. And then there's this *fellow*, David – David Barrington-Jones. He doesn't say much, but he keeps looking at me. One of those bankers is showing him some brochures, but he doesn't seem too interested. Lord Bellforth goes to bed fairly early and Harriet leaves me *in charge* to clear up in the kitchen. Around midnight, just as I'm finishing, there's a knock on the door. It's him – David. He comes in, sits down and says what a marvellous meal and so on. Well of course I'm quite *flattered,* and we chat for a few minutes. Then he asks whether we can meet for a coffee or a drink some time – and, well, you know how it is, George. Here's this *handsome chap*, who they say is a millionaire, asking me if I want to go out with him. And life with Jim is not working out too well. He's spending most of the money – and most of the time – down at the pub, anyway."

George Macey drinks his tea and looks out towards the woods sadly. He's almost certain that he knows what's coming next. Sally *stares* at him.

"I know what you're thinking, George. But look at it from my point of view. A chance in a lifetime! So I *agree*, and things just take their natural course. We meet up, sometimes here, sometimes in a hotel in Durham. I often visit my father there and stay overnight, so that was easy. Jim's mum always looks after the boys when I'm away. And very soon I'm in love with David and he's in love with me. He starts talking about a *divorce.* And money, naturally, is no problem."

Sally Hardcastle looks at Macey and smiles *shyly*. She's still crying a little.

"I know it's wrong, George, but there we are."

Macey grunts and pours another cup of tea.

"And then?" he enquires. But he already knows the answer.

"Then?" says Sally. "About four months later, Jim finds out everything. He checks up with my father and sees me and David together one day in Durham. So he arranges it all! He *exchanges* the guns. I know old Joe Taylor, the gun *steward*, and he doesn't make mistakes. David is killed and later Jim tells me that he saw Lord Bellforth giving David the *faulty* gun. He says he isn't going to tell the police because then he'll lose his job as head *beater*. I don't believe him. Not a word! Lord Bellforth isn't a murderer! It was Jim! So I talk, argue, and then things go from bad to worse. When he's not working, he's drinking. Jim wasn't really a bad man, George. But he couldn't live with the guilt. So I tell him to go to the police and *make a clean breast of it*. Make a *statement*! That was a couple of days ago and the rest – well, you know everything now! Do you want to see his *statement*? I can get it! It's upstairs!"

George Macey makes a decision. He doesn't want to see Jim Hardcastle's *confession*. He doesn't want to know how Jim gave another gun to David on the way to the woods. Quite simply, he doesn't want to know the details. He finishes his tea and walks to the front door.

"Sally, don't *bother*. Just forget it. It's only a piece of paper. Throw it away – or, better, just burn it."

The two boys are still collecting things from the bedroom. He looks back at Sally, who is now clearing away the cups and saucers. Various thoughts flash through his mind: the past, the coal mines, the woods and ducks, the future of Haddington, those damned new-rich investment bankers and old established families like the Bellforths, his job, and all the other jobs! Let it go, he thinks. *Rest in peace*, David Barrington-Jones! *Rest in peace*, Jim Hardcastle! I need a strong whisky and tomorrow the gentlemen need ducks.

The shoot at the weekend is a wonderful *success*. Back in the office, Gordon congratulates George Macey, as does Lord Bellforth.

"You know, it's an awful shame about poor old Jim Hardcastle. Still, accidents do happen, Mr Macey."

"Yes, Your Lordship. You're quite right. Jim's death really WAS an accident."

"What do you mean, Mr Macey?" says Gordon, who is adding up *figures* and working out costs. Macey says nothing and leaves the office. Lord Bellforth rushes out.

"George, what do you mean? Hardcastle's death really WAS an accident!"

They stand in front of the house. Macey turns away and then turns back.

"Well, sir. You remember that other accident a couple of years ago, don't you? Gordon's friend, David Barrington-Jones. The *heir* to Tingworth *Pottery*. That, I'm afraid, was not an accident, my Lord."

Macey tells Bellforth what he knows. From the woods and *ponds* they can hear the quacking of the ducks as the sun begins to set. The *gamekeeper* walks to his car as Lord Bellforth stands by the new, oak doors of Haddington *Manor*. Bellforth seems, again, to be much older. His voice is quiet and *trembling*.

"You know, George. Hardcastle tried to *blackmail* me. That's why I was so..."

Lord Bellforth follows Macey, not quite sure about what is going to happen.

"George, what should we do? Go to the police? Tell me what to do."

The *gamekeeper slams* the car door and opens the window. He feels frustrated and angry.

"Nothing! You can do absolutely nothing, sir! We're going to *let sleeping dogs lie*! But you do understand, don't you? David Barrington-Jones's death wasn't an accident. It was murder, my Lord. It really WAS murder!"

MIDNIGHT IN THE PARK

Anne Ellsworth

Chapter 1: A Note in John Lennon's Shirt Pocket

It is after three o'clock and they have passed the British Royalty, some European ministers and Ronald Reagan. Debbie has shot a whole film of 36 pictures and is getting hungry. But then Scott turns around the next corner and sees the Beatles.

Oh no, she thinks. Now we will never get out of here...

"Oh cool," Scott says excitedly. "The Beatles!"

He walks over to the group of four wax *figures* and *pretends* to shake George Harrison's hand. "Hi, George. *What's up*?"

Debbie rolls her eyes when her husband starts a conversation with Ringo Starr, who just keeps smiling at him. "I guess he doesn't understand American English," Scott says after a while and turns to Paul McCartney. "But I know YOU do, Paul," he says. "So where's Linda? Don't tell me you left her at home? A man should not leave his wife at home, right, Debbie? You never know what trouble she could get herself into..."

Even though she is hungry and tired, she has to smile at him. He is so sweet, funny and *handsome*. She still can *hardly* believe that he is her husband, and that they are on their *honeymoon* here in Old Europe. She must be the luckiest girl in the whole world.

"Hey, John, your *handkerchief* is all *crinkled*. Here, let me *straighten* it *out* for you," Scott now says to John Lennon and *smoothens* the white *handkerchief* in the wax *figure's* shirt pocket. "What did you do last night, old boy?"

Then he turns round. "I have an idea, sweetheart! Why don't you take a picture of me with the Beatles? Dave back home will be *thrilled*! You know that the Beatles are his absolute favourite band!"

"But I can't take any more pictures. I have to buy another film first," Debbie answers. When she sees the disappointed look on his face, she adds, "Tell you what: We will come back tomorrow morning. Let's go get something to eat and a new roll of film. I'm hungry and I want to *freshen up* a bit at the hotel."

"Okay, let's do that," Scott *agrees*. "See you tomorrow, old *buddies*. And don't do anything I wouldn't do!"

On their way out of Madame Tussaud's *Wax Museum* they pass a *figure* in the uniform of the guards sitting on a chair and reading a newspaper. "This one with the big nose looks funny," Scott says and points at the *figure*. "He is a real piece of art. "

The piece of art suddenly *sneezes*, and the whole paper starts to shake. Then the guard *folds up* the newspaper and gets up. He *glances* angrily at the young American who thought he was another wax *figure* and walks out of the room.

"You're right – this one IS a real piece of art! Amazing what modern technology can do these days, isn't it?" Debbie says and laughs.

Übung 1: Lesen Sie weiter und unterstreichen Sie die jeweils richtige Verbform!

Next morning, they (1.) had/are having/have breakfast in the hotel. Debbie has eggs with ham, toast and orange juice, while Scott (2.) tries/try/tried the "Continental Breakfast".

"Sounds great," he says. "I wonder what it is?"

When the waiter serves him two rolls, a few slices of ham and cheese, jam, honey and butter, he says, "But I (3.) order/orders/ ordered a 'Continental Breakfast'."

"That IS a 'Continental Breakfast', sir," the waiter explains. "It's what they (4.) eaten/ate/eat for breakfast on the Continent."
"That's all?" Scott looks disappointed.
Debbie laughs. "What (5.) have/did/does you expect, sweetheart?"
"Well, something special – like steak with *hash browns* or *pancakes with maple syrup*."
"That would (6.) been/being/be an American breakfast, Scott! Don't forget we're in Europe."
"The Europeans are crazy," Scott says while he (7.) is cutting/was cutting/were cutting one of his rolls. "How can a *grown* man live on a breakfast like this?"

An hour later they are back at Madame Tussaud's. Again they pass lots of British *dukes* and *earls* before they get to the Beatles.
"Hi, we're back," Scott says to the group of four wax *figures* as if they can hear him.
Debbie takes out her camera and gets it ready. Scott stands next to John Lennon.
"She loves me, yeah yeah yeah!" he sings into an *invisible* microphone.
"Does she now?" Debbie asks as she starts to take pictures of him with the group of musicians.
"Oh yeah, she loves me, and you know that can't be bad," he sings in reply. Then he looks at her and sends her an kiss through the air that makes her feel very warm, even though this English July is much cooler than summer in Connecticut.
"Did you get that?" he asks.
"I got it all – the photo and the kiss," she answers and smiles at him proudly.
"Maybe we should go back to the hotel," Scott says with a *twinkle* in his eyes. "That breakfast just made me hungry for more..."

She is about to *agree* when she notices something *strange*. “Hey, look at John Lennon’s *handkerchief*!” she says to her husband. “Or IS it a *handkerchief* at all?”
Scott takes a step towards the wax *figure*. “What’s that?” he asks. “Yesterday it was a *handkerchief* – and today it looks like a piece of paper...”
He looks round, but none of the guards are nearby. So he *cautiously* takes the white piece of paper out of John Lennon’s shirt pocket. Then he unfolds it, and together they *stare* at the words written on the paper:

> *Strawberry Tart*,
> The tea is getting too hot over here –
> Meet me in The Park at midnight for an *apple turnover*!
> *Cream Puff*

They put the piece of paper back into the shirt pocket and think about the *strange message*. What can it mean?

Übung 2: Lesen Sie weiter und setzen Sie das Fragewort ***what*** *oder* ***why*** *in die Lücken!*

ÜBUNG 2 !

“‘*Apple turnover*’? Could it be a joke?” Debbie wonders. “It sounds as if someone wants to *turn over* something at midnight. No, I don’t think it is just a joke. It must be something illegal. Or (1.) ___why___ would anyone hide a *message* like this in John Lennon’s shirt?”

"You're right," Scott *agrees*. "But (2.) ___what___ could that be? Drugs? Stolen *goods*?"

"It could be anything," she says. "So (3.) ___what___ shall we do about it?"

Scott thinks hard. "Well, we have to be careful that we don't let the criminals know that we know. Otherwise they will just *turn over* their dirty *goods* somewhere else."

"Good thinking," Debbie *agrees*. "(4.) ___What___ about the guards? Should we let them know about that *strange note*?"

"Better not," Scott says. "(5.) ___What___ if they are part of the gang? Perhaps the *note* is meant for one of them?"

"Well, then we better inform the police. Let's go."

They leave the Beatles behind, make their way past the *earls* and *dukes* and walk towards the exit. There Debbie suddenly stops. "Oh, how stupid of me!" she exclaims. "(6.) ___Why___ didn't I take a picture of that *note*?"

"That would be a good idea," Scott says. "Let's go back."
They turn round and head back inside. Once again they pass the British aristocracy, and Debbie feels as if she is seeing old friends. But when they get to the Beatles and step in front of John Lennon, there is no *note*. They are greeted by the white *handkerchief* that was in his shirt pocket yesterday!
"Wow," Scott says. "Whoever that *note* was for sure was quick!"

Debbie looks around carefully. A guard who was not there earlier suddenly appears near the door. He is *staring* at her and Scott.
"Sweetheart", she whispers, "don't turn around now. One of the guards is watching us!"
"Okay," he *mumbles*. Then he *pretends* to look for something on the floor. "Damn, they're not here either," he says. "I was so sure I still had my sunglasses when we got here!"
"I think you left them at the hotel, sweetheart," Debbie says as the guard *watches* them *closely*. "You know how you always forget to take things along – and then forget that you forgot."
Scott grins at her and kisses her *tenderly*. "But I've got you to remind me, sweets. That's why I married you."
"Oh, is that the only reason?" Debbie asks.
"Well, there is another reason but I can't tell you that one – I can only show you..."
The guard finally looks away, and the two young Americans hurry past him through the doorway and out of the building.
"Wow, that was close," Scott says when they are out in the street.

After a fifteen-minute walk round the centre of London Debbie sees a red *telephone booth*.
"Aren't they pretty?" she says. "Just like in the movies!"
Scott is more interested in where to put what coin and what number to dial. "Is this the same as an *emergency*?" he wonders.
"I don't think so," Debbie answers. "Better look for the regular phone number of a police station."
When Scott finally finds a number listed in the *telephone directory* and picks up the *receiver*, there is no *dial tone*.
"Oh damn," he *curses*. "The phone is broken."
They step outside the *telephone booth*.
"We have to find a policeman," Debbie says.

Ten minutes later they reach Piccadilly Circus. "There is one over there," Scott says and points at a police officer directing traffic. "Let's tell him about the *note*."

"Hey, Bob!" he calls out. The officer does not react. "HEY, BOB!" he calls louder.

The policeman still does not seem to hear him.

"Why do you call him Bob?" Debbie wants to know.

"That's what they're all called over here in England," Scott says. "I saw that in a movie."

"Oh, you mean 'Bobby'," Debbie smiles. "They're called 'Bobby', not Bob!"

"Oh, Bobby – Bob, who cares?" Scott *mumbles*. "It all sounds the same, doesn't it?"

"Excuse me, sir", she calls, "can you help us?"

Now the policeman turns round.

"What do you need, madam? Are you lost?"

She shakes her head. "No, but we have some information you might be interested in."

Then she starts telling him all about the piece of paper in John Lennon's shirt pocket and the *strange message* written on it.

The man *stares* at her. "What?" he asks. "*Cream puffs*? John Lennon's *handkerchief*? *Strawberry tart*? I only know 'Strawberry Fields', madam. That's an old Beatles song. But '*Strawberry tart*'? Why, you must *be mistaken*! I don't quite understand the problem."

"Well, Bob – I mean, sir – we believe that something funny is going on over at that French Madam's *wax museum*," Scott tries to explain. "The *note* sounded as if something is going to be *turned over* at midnight tonight, and we think it must be illegal *goods*. So we wanted to report it."

"*Strawberry tarts* aren't illegal over here, sir," the Bobby says and laughs to himself about these American tourists who come to Lon-

don with the craziest ideas. *Strawberry tarts* indeed!
"We know that, sir," Debbie says. "But we believe it is a *message* with a hidden meaning. And then one of the guards was *watching* us *suspiciously*."
The policeman is too *polite* to tell these two American tourists that he, too, would *watch* them *suspiciously* if they started to look into John Lennon's shirt pocket. Instead he says, "I'm sorry, madam, but I have to take care of the traffic. If you have some *suspicious* observation you want to report, then you need to go to the nearest police station. It's two blocks down on your left. Have a nice day."
And with that he turns round and ignores Scott and Debbie.
"Bob *obviously* isn't going to help us," Scott says. "Come on, let's go."
"What shall we do?" Debbie asks. "Do you think the officers at the police station will believe us?"
"No, actually I don't," he answers. "We'll just have to find out ourselves what that mysterious '*apple turnover*' is all about. But for now, let's go find some place where we can have a second breakfast! Or lunch. Or both. I'm *starving*."

Chapter 2: A Walk in the Park

It is too late in the day for another breakfast, and so they have a *deep-dish pizza* at a fast-food restaurant.
"Mmm, this pizza is delicious," Scott says happily and bites into his third slice. "I wish we had these in the States. This British food isn't too bad after all!"
"That's not British food," Debbie says. "It's Italian – well, not really Italian either. Or do they serve *deep-dish pizza* in Italy?"
"Well, it doesn't matter to me," Scott says. "Why don't we just call it 'continental food'."

Debbie *swallows* her last piece of pizza. "How are we going to find out where and how these illegal *goods* are being *turned over*?" she asks. "All we know is that it will happen in The Park at midnight."

"'The Park' must be Hyde Park," Scott says.

"But where in Hyde Park? It's a pretty large place, isn't it?"

"Yes, I think so," Scott says. "I left the city map in our hotel room, but I looked at it yesterday. Hyde Park is very big. They could meet anywhere there."

"Then it is either a place where they have met before, or the meeting point is hidden in the *message*, too," Debbie thinks aloud.

"What else did it say in the *note*, sweetheart?" Scott asks. "I have forgotten. Wasn't it something about hot tea?"

"Oh yes, you're right! It said something about 'The tea is getting too hot'. So what does that mean?"

"Maybe a *hothouse*?" Scott wonders.

Debbie shakes her head. "It sounds more like a place where they serve tea and cakes – all that stuff about *strawberry* and *cream tarts*..."

"...and *apple turnover*s," Scott says and *nods*.

"A *tearoom,*" Debbie suddenly says. "Of course, that's it – a *tearoom*!"

"Is that something like a coffee shop?"

"Yes, exactly. Only they serve tea instead of coffee. I saw a few along the way," Debbie informs him. "Wake up, sweetheart – we're in England."

"Don't I know it," Scott *mumbles*. "But the pizza is pretty good."

The young American couple spends the afternoon walking around Hyde Park, holding hands and taking pictures of pretty magnolia bushes and each other. When they meet a group of girls in British school uniforms, they ask one of the girls to take a picture of them under a tall *chestnut tree*.

"We're from Connecticut and here on our *honeymoon,*" Debbie explains.

"How romantic!" the girl exclaims, handing the camera back to her. The other girls *giggle* and *glance* at Scott *admiringly*. Debbie thanks the girl with a smile. "Do you perhaps know if there is a *tea-room* nearby?" she asks and adds *innocently*, "we love your English tradition of tea time."

"Yes, actually there is a *tearoom* just past that *bend* over there," the girl answers and points in the direction. "It's right in the middle of some trees, and it's a very pretty spot."

Debbie thanks her again and *proudly* walks off with her *handsome* husband.

"If they only knew what we are REALLY doing here," Scott says. "*Snooping* around the park and looking for a place where some *crooks* are having a secret meeting at midnight..."

"They'd be *thrilled* if they knew," Debbie says.

"Yeah – we're two PDILs on a secret mission," Scott adds. "That means Private Detectives In Love."

Übung 3: Lesen Sie weiter und setzen Sie die richtigen Präpositionen in die Lücken ein!
(of (2x), in, round, for (2x), from (2x))

ÜBUNG 3 !

This explanation earns him a kiss, which *distracts* the two private detectives (1.) ____________ their course of *investigation* for a few minutes. But soon they are back on the job. They walk (2.) ____________ the *bend* the girl showed them and *stumble upon* the prettiest little *tearoom* (3.) ____________ the heart (4.) ____________ the beautiful park. It looks like an old pavilion.

"Oh, how lovely!" Debbie exclaims. "And how romantic!"

"Yes, just the right place (5.) ________________ two PDILs looking (6.) ________________ something delicious to eat," Scott says. "Let's see what kind (7.) _______________ cakes they serve."

Two chocolate tarts, lemon meringues and *cream puffs* later they leave the *tearoom* with the information (8.) ______________ the friendly waitress that this is the only *tearoom* in the park that serves *strawberry tarts* and *cream puffs*.

"So this must be the spot where the meeting will take place tonight," Scott says. "Phew, why did I eat that last *cream puff*? I'm so full I can't walk!"
They decide to go back to the hotel for a rest before starting out on their exciting plan for the night.
"Here you are, sir," the hotel receptionist says, handing Scott the room key. "Are you enjoying your *stay* in London?"
"I certainly am," Scott replies. "What an exciting city it is."
"It's thrilling," Debbie adds, smiling at him, and Scott smiles back at her.
The receptionist thinks how sweet they are – a young couple in love! Of course everything feels thrilling and brand new to them. Ah yes, that's how he felt with Louise five years ago. But now their lives centre around the telly, screaming children and spaghetti stains on the carpet. These days their only thrill is when young Marvin has a new baby tooth. Actually, life in London can be

pretty *dull* when you're not a tourist – or in love.
"Enjoy it while it lasts," he says with a knowing smile.
"Thank you, sir," Scott says. "I think I know how to make it last."
"So how do you know how to make it last?" Debbie asks him on their way up to the room.
"I can't tell you that," he answers. "I can only show you."
But one look into his eyes tells her enough.

They leave their hotel at 8:30 p.m. Both are wearing dark clothes so that they can *melt* into the dark without being seen.
"This gives us enough time for dinner on the way," Scott says.
"Don't you ever stop thinking about food?" Debbie asks.
"Well, yes – on special *occasions*," he responds with a *twinkle* in his eyes. "But that's an *occasion* I can't talk about in public. All I can say is that it's the nicest *occasion* in the world."
Debbie just smiles in agreement. But now it is time to think about the secret mission that is *lying ahead of* them.

Übung 4: Lesen Sie weiter und setzen Sie die passenden Substantive ein!
(dark, feet, restaurant, curries, midnight, park, moon, dinner, park bench)

ÜBUNG 4 !

"So let's find a nice (1.) ____________________ for a bite to eat," she says. "And during (2.) ____________________ we can talk about our plan for tonight."

Scott *nods*. "How about one of those Indian (3.) ______________ they serve here? I think I would like to try one."

About twenty minutes before (4.) ________ Scott and Debbie are back inside the (5.) ________. They walk around in the (6.) ________, looking for the *tearoom*.

"Did we take this path?" Scott whispers. "Everything looks so different in the dark."

"I think we took that one over there. I remember passing a *park bench* and turning left just after it."

They find the (7.) ________ Debbie saw this afternoon and turn left a few (8.) ________ further on.

The *tearoom* appears in front of them, *surrounded by* tall black *shadows* and *illuminated* by a cold silvery (9.) ________.

"It doesn't seem so cosy now, does it?" Scott says quietly.
"Not really," Debbie whispers. "But I think we should be quiet now and hide behind the *hedges* over there. They may *show up* early."
"Good thinking," Scott whispers back. *Cautiously* they *sneak* over to the bushes and disappear behind them.
Scott holds his arm into the moonlight and looks at his watch: 11:47 p.m. If he and Debbie are right, then something will happen right in front of their eyes in a few minutes. He wonders what the "apple" could be that will be *turned over* at midnight. Something big like stolen *goods*? A suitcase full of jewellery or money? Or some small package? Like a few pounds of cocaine or heroin? Luckily Debbie has her camera with her. Of course she can't use the *flash* – the criminals would surely see it *going off*. But the moonlight might be *bright* enough to get something on film.
Another glance at his watch tells him that it is now 11:51 p.m. Deb-

bie looks at him. He holds up nine fingers and she *nods*. Nine more minutes till midnight!
Six minutes before midnight Scott sees something moving in the dark. It is *sneaking* up from behind the trees. When it comes closer, he can see that it is a man dressed in black clothes. He touches Debbie's arm and points silently at the *figure*. *Breathlessly* they both watch the man come closer, until he stops by the nearest tree. He leans against the tree and *glances* at his watch.
Two minutes before midnight they hear a noise. The man seems to hear it, too, because he turns his head in the direction of where it came from. Now there is a second movement in the dark.
Scott points at the camera Debbie is holding in her hand. She *nods* and holds it up, ready to take pictures.

Übung 5: Lesen Sie weiter und unterstreichen Sie das jeweils passende Verb!

ÜBUNG 5 !

A second *figure* is (1.) going/coming/appearing closer to the little teahouse. It is a woman with blond hair that (2.) shows/shines/*beams* in the moonlight. She is (3.) holding/handing/keeping a dark bundle in her arms. Debbie starts (4.) making/getting/taking pictures. Fortunately no one can (5.) listen/hear/see the quiet clicking of her digital camera.
The two *strangers* (6.) start/get/stop whispering to each other. Scott (7.) goes/tries/will to listen but he can only *overhear* the words "too many questions". He guesses that someone must be asking too many questions about that bundle – whatever it is. What (8.) would/will/could it be? Pounds of drugs *wrapped up* in some dark *cloth*, so that it looks like a coat that the woman is carrying in her arms? In case she is stopped by one of those Bobs in police uniform?

Chapter 3: Matches Without Cigarettes

Debbie's camera is clicking away.

After a few minutes the blond woman lifts her arms and hands over the bundle to the man. In that second Debbie can see a small *pale* face in the bundle. She is so shocked she almost forgets to take more pictures. It is a baby.

The bundle is a baby. The woman is handing a baby over to that *stranger* in black clothes.

Why would a mother hand her small child over to a man in Hyde Park in the middle of the night? That is, IF that is the baby's mother.

And what if she ISN'T the baby's mother? What if this is not her own child?

Could this be the "stolen *goods*"? A baby? Somebody else's baby?

Scott is *staring* at the man now holding the bundle. The *stranger* *nods* to the woman. Then he disappears between the trees with the bundle.

Scott looks at Debbie with a questioning look in his eyes. He couldn't see what was in the bundle, so Debbie *pretends* to *cradle* a baby in her arms.

He *stares* at her for a moment; then he slowly *nods*. He understands what she is trying to tell him.

The blond woman turns in the other direction and disappears behind the trees...

"Come on," Scott whispers to Debbie. "Let's follow her."

They creep out of the bush and *sneak* over the grass to the trees. The woman is about fifty *yards* ahead of them. Her blond hair is *illuminated* by the *pale* moonlight. Now she turns round the *bend*.

"Come on, hurry!" Scott whispers, holding Debbie's hand. "We don't want to lose her!"

Übung 6: Unterstreichen und übersetzen Sie die sieben Adjektive im nächsten Abschnitt!

Debbie hurries along round the *bend* and past the *park bench*. The woman is walking quickly across a wide *lawn*. The young Americans have to keep close to the tall trees so the woman can't see them. But suddenly Debbie *stumble*s over a dead *branch* that is lying on the ground. It cracks. Before the woman can turn round to see what caused the sudden noise, Scott pulls Debbie down to the soft ground.

When the woman DOES turn round, she sees two lovers in a *tender embrace* who only have eyes for each other.

"Did I ever tell you how much I love you?" Scott murmurs as he kisses Debbie's neck.

"You did – but feel free to tell me again," Debbie whispers as she strokes his neck.

"Well, let me see – as much as there is water in the ocean, as much as there is sand on the beach..."

The woman stops for a moment, watches them, and hurries away.

"Oh damn," Scott says, getting up quickly. "Looks like we lost her."

They hurry on, but the woman has disappeared behind some magnolia bushes at the end of the *lawn*.

1. ______________ 5. ______________

2. ______________ 6. ______________

3. ______________ 7. ______________

4. ______________

Scott and Debbie *sneak* through the bushes, but the woman is gone. "She could have turned anywhere – left or right or straight ahead,"

Scott says helplessly. "There are too many trees and bushes all around!"

Then Debbie feels something soft *brush* against her hand in the dark. When she turns to see what it is, she finds a woollen *garment* hanging on a *branch*.

"Look, Scott – a jacket!" she whispers and holds it up to the moonlight.

Scott looks at it. "Hey, I think that's HER jacket. She must have lost it when she hurried away!"

"What a piece of good luck for us – and *bad luck* for her," Debbie says. "Now the police may be able to find her."

"Let's see if there is anything in the pockets", Scott *suggests,* "like a letter with an address, a phone number or something else that could identify her."

Excitedly Debbie searches through the first pocket and comes up with three *matchboxes*.

"What's that?" Scott asks. "Oh, just *matchboxes*! Well, that's not going to tell us anything, is it? Let's see what's in the other pocket."

Nothing. The other pocket is empty.

"Three *matchboxes*, and no cigarettes?" Scott wonders. "What does that mean? A non-smoker who likes to burn down houses?"

"A non-smoking *arsonist*? That's pretty good, Sherlock Holmes," Debbie says and grins. "But look, the name and address of a pub is printed on these *matchboxes*. What could that mean?"

"I have no idea," Scott says and *shrugs*. "A beer-drinking, non-smoking *arsonist*?"

Now Debbie notices that the jacket smells of smoke. "It smells of cigarette smoke," she says. "What about a waitress? A waitress who works at that pub? A waitress would have *matchboxes* in her pocket even if she doesn't smoke."

Scott gives her a surprised look.

Übung 7: Beantworten Sie die Fragen zum Text in vollständigen Sätzen!

1. What is in the bundle?

2. What does Debbie stumble over?

3. What did the woman leave behind?

4. How many matchboxes does Debbie find?

5. What is printed on the matchboxes?

6. What does Debbie notice?

"A pub waitress? Yeah, that sounds good to me. You're pretty smart, you know. Actually that's one of the reasons why I married you."
"Oh yes? And what's the other reason?" she asks with a smile.
"I can't tell you – but just wait until we're back at the hotel, then I'll show you."
Since the non-smoking blond waitress has disappeared anyway, they take a few minutes for a long kiss before they decide what to do next.
"So what now?" Debbie asks, a bit out of breath.

"Well, I know what I would REALLY like to do... but first we have to notify the police, don't we?" Scott replies.
"Do you think they will believe us now?"
"They have to – we are eye *witnesses* to the turnover of a helpless little apple. We also have pictures of the crime, and even the jacket of one of the criminals. Plus a *clue* about her identity! Hey, we're pretty good PDILs, aren't we?"
"The best," Debbie says.

They are back in the streets of London, looking for a police station.
"If we call them, they may not understand what we are telling them", Scott says, "so it's better we go there in person."
Debbie *nods*. "Then we can also show them the pictures I took with my camera," she says.
After they have walked for a while, Debbie turns to two women passing by. "Excuse me", she says, "can you tell me where the nearest police station is?"
One of the women shakes her head. "Sorry, but we don't live here. We're just tourists from Glasgow."
They walk on. A few *yards* further on Scott points at a group of people. "How about asking them?"
Debbie hurries on to *catch up with* them. "Excuse me", she calls, "can you help us? We're looking for the nearest police station!"
The people turn round. They are Japanese tourists with cameras. They shake their heads, smile *politely* and walk on.
"What about that couple across the street?" Scott asks. "Maybe THEY are Londoners!"
They quickly cross the street and stop the two *strangers*. "Excuse me, sir, can you tell me the way to the nearest police station?" Scott asks the man.
"Sorry, can't help you there," the man says, smiling. He is wearing

a very colourful shirt with flowers all over. "We're American like you. We're just here on vacation."
"Another American couple – how nice," his wife says. She looks at Debbie and adds, "We're from Milwaukee. And where are you from?"
"Connecticut. We're on our *honeymoon*."
The woman turns to her husband. "They're on their *honeymoon*! Isn't that romantic? Say, would you like to join us? We're looking for a nice bar or pub."

Übung 8: Lesen Sie weiter und unterstreichen Sie jeweils das sinnvollste Wort!

ÜBUNG 8 !

(1.) And/But/Because Scott and Debbie don't have any time for small talk or a drink. (2.) "Lucky/Sorry/Why, we have to find a police station first," Debbie apologizes.
"Hopefully there's (3.) nothing/nobody/nowhere wrong? Can we help you in any (4.) type/way/method?"
"No, thanks. I just need a *stamp* for my passport," Scott says quickly, hoping they won't wonder why he needs a *stamp* for his passport in the (5.) middle/medium/centre of the night.
"Oh, that's (6.) also/not/too bad! Well, maybe some other time," the American woman says. "(7.) Good/Much/Plenty luck! Nice to meet you!"

"Aren't there any people from London in London?" Scott asks when they walk on. "No Londoners and no British food – what a *strange* city."
Finally they are lucky. A taxi driver gives them the directions to a police station that is only a few *yards* away in an *alley*.

"So this is where these Bobs are hiding", Scott *mumbles*, "in a dark *alley* so nobody can find them."

But this time they find a police officer on *night shift* who listens to their story – *cream puffs* and all. "That sounds like a serious crime," he says. "Are you certain you saw a baby?"

"Yes, and the poor thing looked as if it was sleeping," Debbie answers. "But I don't know if it was sleeping – I sure hope it was still alive."

"No one has reported a kidnapping or a missing baby in this city," the police officer informs them. "But then who would hand a small child over to someone else at night in the park?"

"And don't forget the *strange note* we found in John Lennon's shirt pocket," Scott reminds him. "That sounded *fishy* from the start."

The policeman *nods*. "There's something *fishy* going on alright. I will inform Scotland Yard right away. Please don't do any more *investigations* on your own. We will most certainly take care of the matter. Could you stop by Scotland Yard Headquarters tomorrow morning? They will need official *statements* from you both. Oh – and could you leave that camera here? You can pick it up at the Yard tomorrow. We want to have a look at the photos."

They also have to leave the jacket and the three *matchboxes* at the police station. By the time they step back out into the *alley*, it is after one o'clock in the morning.

"Are you tired? Do you want to go back to the hotel?" Scott asks. "Or do you feel like I do?"

"How do you feel?" Debbie asks.

"Hungry – for a midnight snack. And for more adventures. What was the name of the pub on those *matchboxes* again?"

"The Golden Lion," Debbie replies with a smile.

That is one of the reasons why she loves Scott so much. Because he thinks and feels exactly like her.

Chapter 4: The Golden Lion

Übung 9: Bestimmter oder unbestimmter Artikel? Lesen Sie weiter und unterstreichen Sie die richtige Variante!

ÜBUNG 9 !

They take (1.) the/a taxi to (2.) the/a pub. After a short ride through *bright* streets and (3.) a/the few dark *alleys* (4.) a/the taxi stops in front of (5.) a/the house with a sign that reads "The Golden Lion". Two big golden lions sit to (6.) a/the left and right of (7.) a/the door.

"What do we do if she is here?" Scott asks. "I mean she saw us in the park. What will we do if she recognizes us?"
Debbie shakes her head. "I am sure she didn't see our faces."
"But perhaps she saw our clothes? Then she may remember the couple in the park..."
"I'll just *take off* my jacket. Why don't you *take off* your sweat-shirt? Didn't you put on a t-shirt as well?"
Scott *nods*. "Yes, I did. Good thinking! Let's do that."
Debbie quickly takes off her jacket and Scott pulls off his sweat-shirt.

The pub is hot, loud and filled with smoke. Even though it is late, the place is full of people talking and drinking and singing along to the music. A group of four men are playing cards at a table in the corner. One of them has just lost the last game.
"Oops, looks like the next round's on you, Benny, old *chap*!" one of the other three calls out.
Benny promptly waves at the barkeeper, points at his beer glass and holds up four fingers. The barkeeper *nods*.
"I think we just saw our first real Londoners," Scott says.
But Debbie is more interested in finding a place where she can sit

down. Her legs hurt from walking around the city all day, and she is starting to feel tired. So she looks for an empty table and suddenly sees the American couple from Milwaukee. They are sitting at a small round table near the bar, and there are two more chairs that don't seem to be taken by anyone.

"Look who's sitting over there – the Americans we asked for directions! Why don't we sit down with them?" she *suggests,* and without waiting for Scott's reply, she starts to walk over to their table.

The two American tourists from Milwaukee welcome them happily and make room at their small table.

"How nice to see you again!" the woman says. "Were you able to take care of the problem with your passport? By the way, I'm Mildred, and this is my husband, Bob."

When Scott comes back from the bar with two glasses of ale, Bob starts telling his new friend about his job as an *undertaker,* while Mildred smiles and *nods* enthusiastically.

"The business has been in our family for generations, and I'm *proud* of it", Bob says, "even though a lot of people don't like my kind of work. But why is that? After all, I'm just serving the *deceased* and their loved ones, right?"

Scott *nods* at him. Bob gets up and goes to the men's room. Scott rolls his eyes. "This Bob is almost as bad as that British Bob," he whispers to Debbie. "Do we have to sit with these people?"

"They're our perfect *cover,*" she whispers back, *sipping* her ale. "If the waitress comes back, she will never recognize us when she sees us with two other tourists."

"You're right. But Bob is telling me all about his work. It's horrible!"

"Just talk to him while I try to find out something about our waitress," Debbie says.

Two minutes later Bob comes back from the men's room and sits

down again. "Have I told you the secret of my *success* yet?"
"No, but I'm sure you will," Scott replies unhappily.
"It's all in how you prepare the *corpse*," Bob explains.
"Oh really?" Scott says *politely*.
"Yes, how you dress the *deceased* and the make-up you use. My *corpses* always wear just a bit of lipstick and have rosy cheeks – it makes their loved ones really happy," he says, emptying his glass of ale while Scott gives Debbie a *desperate* glance.
Debbie waves at the only waitress working in the pub. It is not the blond woman. This waitress has short red hair. It takes her a while to get round to them because she has to serve all the other tables as well. Debbie knows that the waitress is in a hurry, so she must be quick if she wants to find out anything interesting about a blond woman who might work here.
When the waitress finally comes to their table, Debbie orders another round of drinks and asks, "Don't you have another waitress working here? The other night a blond waitress was serving our table – or have I *mixed* that *up with* another pub?"
The red-haired waitress *nods* and smiles at her.
"No, you're right. We do have another waitress who works here. Her name is Doreen but she left early tonight because she had a terrible toothache. So now I have to take care of all the guests by myself, but I'll *manage*."
"Well, I expect you're glad when the night is over," Debbie responds. "All this running around must make you tired – and then all that smoke in the air must *be* really *hard on* you!"
"Well, I smoke myself, so it's not that bad for me."
"Yes, I guess it's not that bad for smokers," Debbie says and *nods*. "But that other waitress doesn't smoke, does she? I remember her saying something about the terrible smoke from all those cigarettes..." Debbie adds with a questioning look on her face.

ÜBUNG 10 !

Übung 10: Lesen Sie weiter und setzen Sie die Präpositionen in die Lücken ein!
(of (2x), for, in, to (2x), about, at, on)

"Oh yes, you're right", the waitress *agrees*, "it's really hard (1.) ____________ poor Doreen. She doesn't smoke and she's always *complaining* (2.) ____________ how her clothes and her hair smell (3.) ________ smoke (4.) ________ the end (5.) ________ the evening. She says we should get paid extra (6.) ________ having to work (7.) ____________ such a smoky place. But tell that (8.) ________ the boss! Oh well, I've got to get back (9.) ________ work – so it's two more ales and two white wines, right?"

Debbie smiles and nods, and the woman hurries off to the card players. They want to pay their bill and leave.
Debbie turns to Scott. "We will have to give her an extra large *tip*," she whispers into his ear. "She just informed me that there IS a blond waitress who works here. The blond waitress's name is Doreen. She *claimed* to have a toothache and left early tonight."
Scott looks at her with big eyes. "You found all that out just by talking to the waitress? Wow, you're good!"
"I know," Debbie says, grinning at him. "Oh yeah, and one more thing: Doreen doesn't smoke."

A short time later the door opens. Two men enter the pub and sit down at the table which the card players have just left.
Debbie notices that one of the men looks around while the other

one is trying to talk to the red-haired waitress. The waitress shakes her head. Then she turns round and *glances suspiciously* at Debbie. Now she is looking at the man again, shaking her head and walking off to another table.

The man turns to his *companion* and *shrugs*. He says something to the other man, who gets up and walks over to the bar.

"Those two look like undercover police officers," Debbie whispers to Scott. "And I think they just asked the waitress about another waitress who works here, who is blond and a non-smoker."

"How do you know?"

"Well, I was watching them. It looked as if the waitress got *suspicious*. First I asked her about Doreen, and now two *strangers* come in and start asking her the same questions! And it seems that they didn't get any answers from her."

Scott looks at the man at the bar. "I think he wants to make sure that the waitress can't warn the barkeeper. Who knows? Maybe this second waitress is *involved* in the crime, too – or even the barkeeper!"

"...who could warn Doreen, who, in turn, could warn the man she handed the baby over to..." Debbie speculates.

"Right. And that's what these men must be thinking, too, if they are police officers," Scott *agrees*.

"But we've got the information they need, so how are we going to let them know about Doreen?" Debbie wonders.

Scott thinks hard. "What if I drink up this ale and go over to the bar to order another one? Right next to that Sherlock Holmes? That way no one will get *suspicious* – neither the waitress nor the barkeeper."

"Great idea," Debbie *agrees*.

Scott empties his glass and gets up. "I just love this English ale," he says aloud to Bob. "I'm going to get another one from the bar. Shall I bring you one, too?"

It seems to surprise Bob how quickly his new friend can empty a glass of beer. “No, thanks,” he says and shakes his head. “But you should watch your drinking, Buddy, or you may need my business sooner than you think!”
Scott *grimaces* and hurriedly leaves the table. Debbie quickly turns away from the American couple because she is *overcome by a sudden fit of laughter*.

ÜBUNG 11

! *Übung 11: Übersetzen Sie folgende Sätze ins Deutsche!*

1. The card players want to pay their bill and leave.

____

2. We will have to give her a large tip.

____

3. It looked as if the waitress got suspicious.

____

4. What if I drink up this ale?

____

5. That way no one will get suspicious.

____

6. Scott grimaces and hurriedly leaves the table.

____

The young American stands next to the man at the bar. He orders another ale – his third beer in one hour – and *glances* at the *stranger*. Yes, he looks like an undercover policeman. And he acts

like one, too. He seems to be observing everything that is going on. When the barkeeper puts the glass of ale down on the *counter*, Scott thanks him and pays for it. But he cannot leave yet.
"Nice place," he says to the man next to him. "We don't have pubs like this in the States."
"You don't?" the man replies *politely*, without sounding interested in any pubs they have in the States.
"No, man – in the States they have *hardly* any places left where people can smoke," Scott explains. "It must be *hard on* the waitress to work in a place like this if she doesn't smoke."
The man *glances* at him as if he just said something interesting. "Oh yes?"
"Yeah, well, you know how non-smokers feel about cigarette smoke. You see that red-haired waitress over there?" Scott asks, looking in her direction.
"Yes – what about her?"
"Well, she just told my wife that she herself doesn't *mind* the smoke in this place. But there is another waitress who usually works here – a blond waitress named Doreen. And that one is a nonsmoker. And she really *minds* all that cigarette smoke in here. But she left early tonight. She *claimed* to have a toothache."
The man *stares* at him. "She did, did she? And her name is Doreen?" he asks quietly. "Well, *fancy that*! Thanks a lot, sir – I'm sure we can make her toothache go away!"
Scott just *nods*, takes his glass of ale and goes back to the table.
"Did it work?" Debbie whispers excitedly when he sits down again.
"*Sure did*," he informs her. "The man said they could make her toothache go away."
"Who has a toothache?" Bob wants to know. "My brother is a *dentist*, and his secret of *success* is..."
While the first undercover police officer *keeps an eye on* the red-

haired waitress, the man at the bar disappears with the barkeeper in the back of the pub. Nothing else happens.

Fifteen minutes later Scott pays their bill, giving the friendly waitress a large *tip*. Then they say goodbye to the *undertaker* and his wife.

"You must come see us if you're ever in Milwaukee," Bob says. "I'm in the *Yellow Pages*; just look under *undertakers* for Bob Bailey's Last *Farewell* – that's my business."

"I'm sure we will," Scott says.

"I'm sure we never will," he says when they step outside the pub. "Knowing Bob, he may show me how he prepares his *corpses* – rosy cheeks and all. What a horrible thought!"

ÜBUNG 12 !

Übung 12: Lesen Sie weiter und unterstreichen Sie die richtige Variante!

"All's well that ends well," the officer says as he shows Scott and Debbie into a small room at Scotland Yard Headquarters. "You two did a (1.) fine/hard/big job."

Then he tells them the rest of the story. The night before, the two men at the pub got Doreen's (2.) total/whole/full name and address from the barkeeper. They quickly sent two policemen to her address, where she was picked up and brought (3.) into/for/at the station. When she was *questioned* about the baby, she (4.) fell/*stumbled*/broke down and told them (5.) anything/everything/something she knew. She played only a small part in a large criminal organization. The organization *smuggled* babies (6.) of/from/by Russia, Asia and Africa into England. Then they sold the babies to rich Europeans who (7.) shouldn't/wouldn't/couldn't have children of their own and desperately wanted to *adopt* a baby.

"They are all told that their baby is an *orphan*, but in reality these children have been taken away from their homes and families. We will have to find out where these babies are from so we can give them back to their real parents," the officer tells them. "But the waitress Doreen helped us greatly. She gave us a list of names and phone numbers – all the people who were part of that gang. By the way, the barkeeper was one of them as well, and so was one of the guards at Madame Tussaud's. You really were a great help to us, I must say. And now comes the best part: As a sign of our *gratitude* to you we have arranged an *invitation* to Buckingham Palace. Her Majesty Queen Elizabeth wants to meet you and thank you in person."

"Wow!" Scott says. "We're invited by the Queen of England?"

"Yes, sir," the man says, smiling. "You will get a written *invitation* soon. Oh yes, before I forget: The 'Times' called to say they want to interview you for tomorrow's title story. Can you be at your hotel at two o'clock this afternoon? They are sending a team of reporters and photographers over to your hotel."

Scott and Debbie are *thrilled*. They are invited to Buckingham Palace and are even going to be on the *cover* of the "Times"!

"Just one thing, sir," Scott says to the Scotland Yard Officer.

"Yes, what is it?"

"Could you send a copy of tomorrow's 'Times' over to that Bob who directs the traffic at Piccadilly Circus? And a *strawberry tart* as well?"

The officer looks at him in surprise. "Yes, of course – but why?"

"Oh, just tell him it's from the two crazy American tourists who looked into John Lennon's shirt pocket," Scott says with that *twinkle* in his eyes that Debbie loves so much.

LEARNING BY KILLING

Michael Bacon

Chapter 1: Check-In

Tracy Dean, the secretary, smiles at the young man.
"Now, what's your name?"
He must be French, she thinks. He's wearing a raincoat in the middle of July – and he's looking at the women in the corner of the room. The young man laughs loudly and grins at Tracy.
"My name? – Pierre! Pierre Leclerc, of course!"
His teeth are perfectly white and his long, black hair *matches* his deep, brown eyes. The two women in the corner *giggle* and *stare* at Pierre Leclerc. He *shrugs* his shoulders and they *giggle* again.
"Well, Pierre, your class is B1. Your teacher is Jim Ryan. Would you like a cup of coffee? Join the others over there. They're in your class too. Next please!"
A short, rather *plump* man *shuffles* forward. He's wearing *glasses*.
"My name is Mr Schultze. I am a German. Do you want my passport?"
"No", says Tracy, "that isn't necessary, Mr Schultze. You're on my list – and you're in Jim Ryan's class as well. Follow Pierre and have a cup of coffee. By the way, we always use first names here at Church Hill. My name is Tracy – and yours?"
Mr Schultze *hesitates* and then almost whispers.
"It's Karl. Karl with a K!"
"Pleased to meet you, Karl. How was your journey?"
Karl Schultze takes a step backwards. He is a little uncertain about the question. The flight from Hanover to London was punctual, efficient and cheap. The Underground from Heathrow to Waterloo

Station was also cheap, but with two heavy suitcases and three changes it was, quite honestly, unpleasant. The train to Eastcastle was late and slow, with too many people. The taxi from the station was fast, much too fast, and also very expensive. Can he say all this in one sentence or does he need his dictionary? He doesn't want to *offend* Tracy, who is very attractive – and very friendly. Karl remembers a phrase from his English class in Gifhorn!
"Let's cut it short!" he laughs. "My journey was excellent."
Tracy *ticks off* Karl's name and points to the corner with the coffee. Karl, pleased with himself, walks towards the girls. He puts down his two suitcases, takes a cup of coffee and then studies his dictionary.
Tracy Dean continues to note all the new arrivals and send them to the tables with coffee and tea. In all, there are twenty students who want to stay for three weeks at The Church Hill School for English. Three weeks in Eastcastle, a little village on the South Coast. It is not very far from Brighton, about fifteen minutes by train, and the beaches and the cliffs are superb.

Übung 1: Welche Gegenteile gehören zusammen? Ordnen Sie zu!

ÜBUNG 1 !

1. laugh	☐ terrible
2. plump	☐ light
3. whisper	☐ cry
4. cheap	☐ slow
5. late	☐ shout
6. short	☐ expensive
7. superb	☐ slim
8. heavy	☐ tall
9. fast	☐ early

The school is a large Victorian building with a long garden at the back and a *drive* at the front. There's one car parked near the steps that lead to the front door. But what a car! A Rolls Royce from the late fifties! It *sparkles* in the afternoon sunshine. This is the pride and joy of Colonel Lessons, the owner of Church Hill School for English. He's a retired army officer and he *runs* his school with military precision. However, he doesn't appear in the building too often. Most of the time he's at the 19th hole of Eastcastle's Golf Club. This expression is often *confusing* for foreign students. Golf? Aren't there only 18 holes! That's quite right, but people often call the club house the 19th hole or the "watering hole". This is where you can relax and have a drink – or two, or three and often even more.

Occasionally the Colonel comes to the school to check the *accounts* and the reservations for the next course. When he leaves, he raises his hand in *mock* salute and always shouts: "Any problems, call me on the mobile. I'll be at Number 19." Then he marches down the steps and gets into his car. He looks at the clean interior, wipes a few *specks* of dust off the passenger seat and, like a small boy opening a Christmas present, he switches on the engine. He listens carefully. No, he can't hear a thing, so all is in order. A "Roller", he says to himself, is a car that must be seen and not heard. What a marvellous life! All the summer courses are full. This language school business is *money for old rope*! The students pay the exorbitant *fees* before they start; the teachers receive their meagre salary four weeks after their teaching finishes. It's all in the contracts. And the difference between what comes in and what goes out lands in my bank *account*. In about five years I'll be a millionaire! I can move to the South of France and forget this stupid little town for ever! And then he glides off to the golf club and his first gin and tonic of the day.

Tracy is a very attractive woman in her mid-thirties. She's taller than Colonel Lessons and has long, blond hair and a healthy, sun-tanned *complexion*. This comes from her interest in sailing. When she's not at Church Hill you can almost always find her at the harbour, working on her small yacht.

Like all sailors, *male* or female, she spends more time painting and cleaning her boat than actually sailing. She's a native of Eastcastle and loves the relaxed atmosphere of a small, coastal town. The fishing boats, the promenade with its terraced houses and shops, the three pubs for the tourists, the seagulls screeching over the small pier, the *Punch and Judy show* next to the entrance.

Yes, she says to herself, when she's cleaning a railing or washing down the deck, this is heaven on earth! And the job is marvellous, I can't complain at all. Well, except for the boss. Tracey doesn't really like the Colonel. She's fairly sure that he only *run*s the school to make a profit. He's a businessman! But there are always fresh faces. Every summer new students, as well as new teachers. Colonel Lessons has only one permanent member of *staff* – and this is his daughter, Rose. All the other teachers are looking for summer work; they are often people who want to earn a little extra money teaching their mother tongue – sometimes teachers who are between jobs. Occasionally a *con-man* who has no idea how to teach the language but needs the money. For example Henry, last year. A sad *case*, in fact a complete and total failure. But – so it goes. Not everyone can be like Jim Ryan, the new Irish recruit for this summer. His contract is for two courses, six weeks in all. The second course is just beginning. This Sunday, as she begins to paint the mast, Tracy thinks about the changes in her life during the last three weeks. In fact, she's in love with Jim Ryan. OK, it is true that he is a little younger than she is – 29, in fact – but he's so romantic. This may be her last chance.

Übung 2: Welches Wort ist das „schwarze Schaf“? Unterstreichen Sie das nicht in die Reihe passende Wort!

1. attractive, ugly, beautiful, handsome
2. yacht, boat, car, ship
3. building, house, school, garden
4. leave, depart, arrive, glide off
5. clever, stupid, silly, ridiculous
6. sailor, secretary, soldier, officer
7. small, tiny, miniature, huge
8. pier, seagull, harbour, coastal town
9. menu, receipt, food, recipe
10. students, teacher, sailor, pupils

Rose, Colonel Lessons's daughter, is giving a *pep talk* to the *staff.*
"Now, we're all here. The students are here as well. Teaching begins on Monday and, as you know, the motto of Church Hill is 'Learning by Doing'. Each of you has five students and we expect a presentation, in the widest sense of the word, after the three weeks of teaching. You all have a theme. Yours, Terry, is 'English Food', are you happy with that?"
Terry *nods* and makes a few *notes*.
"I'll *manage*," he says. "We can put a menu together that covers everything. With prices and *recipes*. No problem!"
Rose continues.
"Janet, your group must concentrate on music. Anything connected with music. And Patricia – or do you prefer Pat?"
Patricia Jones *shrugs* her shoulders. Rose smiles.
"OK – Pat! Your theme is 'The Village Fair'. You know, the standard stuff about *jumble sales*, *sack races* and so on."
Patricia Jones feels uncomfortable. She comes from Sunderland in

the North-East of England. "The Village Fair" or "The Village Fête" seems to be a very middle-class topic. Typical for the South Coast!

"Rose, that's a very *tall order*. I'll *manage* somehow – but what about Jim?"

Rose turns to Jim Ryan, pauses and takes a deep breath.

"Jim, you know Church Hill's motto. 'Learning by Doing'. We want to change it slightly for your theme. You must produce a short drama with the title 'Learning by Killing'. So, it's *obviously* a rather violent play. But remember – it is a play! We don't want the local police *involved*!"

Übung 3: Lesen Sie weiter und unterstreichen Sie alle Verben im folgenden Textabschnitt!

ÜBUNG 3 !

The four teachers smile and laugh a little. Jim Ryan looks around. "Rose, all of you. I come from Ireland. That means I know all about violence, murder and so on. Not personally, of course. But I think, with a little bit of imagination, I can produce a short play. Dramatic but short! It *depends on* the students I have, naturally."

The others clap their hands. Rose's mobile rings.

"Ah, there's the boss-man. My father's ringing to find out whether everything's going smoothly. OK. *Let's call it a day*. See you all tomorrow. Remember! Monday, 9 a.m. sharp!"

The teachers for the Summer School of 2005 collect their *notes*, smiling, laughing and ready to achieve their *objectives*.

Down at the harbour, Tracy finishes painting the mast. She looks up at the cliffs. On the highest cliff she sees the castle. It must be at

least 800 years old. The stone is grey but, in the sunlight, now seems very white. The seagulls are still screeching. And this is England, she thinks. The England I love. And Jim Ryan? He's not English – he's Irish. But that doesn't matter. Tracy goes back to her car, singing a well-known sea shanty quietly to herself.
"Where have you been all the day, Billy Boy, Billy Boy, where have you been all the day, my Billy Boy? Oh, I've been walking all the day with my darling Nancy Grey, and my Nancy *tickled my fancy*, oh my darling Nancy Grey."
Billy Boy and Nancy Grey, she thinks. Or Jimmy Ryan and Tracy Dean?
The sun begins to set on Eastcastle. The English Channel shimmers in the background. One of the large Dover car ferries, a *speck* on the horizon, is moving slowly towards France. Four or five yachts are returning to the harbour after a day's sailing. The weather forecast is positive. Can anything, anything at all, disturb this *tranquillity*?

Chapter 2: Departure Lounge

"Good morning, ladies and gentlemen!"
Jim Ryan sees five students sitting in the room. They're all a little nervous in their first lesson.
Pierre Leclerc is talking to Elke, a young lady from Zurich. Elke has long blond hair, very large blue eyes and a *figure* that Pierre is *familiar with* from magazines. Pierre is certain that Elke is a model who needs to learn English. He flashes his white teeth and shakes his head of dark hair.
Karl Schultze is sitting at his *desk*. In front of him he has a folder, two pencils and a *biro*. The *biro* is blue – not black and not red. His

dictionary is in his *briefcase*, which stands *proudly* next to the *desk*. Karl adjusts his *glasses* and looks at Mr Ryan, ready and waiting. Next to him is Franka from Spain. A very beautiful woman – with red hair! A redhead! From Spain? Yes, indeed. She can't speak English very well but she can produce a beautiful "th" – the others always *splutter*, particularly Karl. The fifth student is Mahdi. He comes from Oman. He's not interested in the girls, the women, the ladies! He wants to learn English. He wants to be *successful* and develop his country. English! THE language! The "lingua franca" of globalisation. Or is it globalization? He makes a mental *note* to ask the teacher later.

Jim Ryan stands in front of the class. He pauses, and then says:

"My name is Jim. Jim Ryan – and what's your name?"

He goes round the class. They all introduce themselves. Pierre gives his name and laughs. Karl gives his name and *stares*. Elke and Franka say their names very clearly. Mahdi is the only person who introduces himself formally.

"Teacher, I am Mahdi – from Oman. My country needs people who speak good English. I am here to learn English. I like fish and chips. Thank you very much."

Mahdi *bows modestly* and sits down.

Jim Ryan opens his notebook. "So, we have a Pierre, a Karl, an Elke, a Franka and a Mahdi. That's good, very good. Do you know why?"

This question is met with *blank* faces.

"OK, I'll tell you why. We're going to learn English in the next three weeks. 'Learning by Doing' is the motto of Church Hill School. And we, you five students and myself, are going to produce a play. Not a comedy, not a tragedy – just a simple murder story. 'Learning by Doing' may be the motto of Church Hill, but the title of our little play is 'Learning by Killing'!"

ÜBUNG 4 !

Übung 4: Enträtseln Sie die folgenden Definitionen!

1. A newspaper with lots of pictures: ______________________ (agzanemi)
2. A small table where you can work: ______________ (edks)
3. Something you can write with: ______________ (oibr)
4. A bag for carrying papers and books: ______________________ (sefibcrae)
5. Something you organize your papers in: ______________ (rlfdoe)
6. Pieces of fried potato: ______________ (ichsp)
7. A person with red hair: ______________________ (ahddeer)
8. A group of pupils or students who are taught and study together: ____________________ (saslc)

Jim Ryan begins to hand out some sheets of paper.
"Now, I know that all of you have about two or three years of English behind you. That means that we have to keep the dialogue in this play fairly simple. Its *success depends on*... Yes, Mahdi. You've got a question. That's good. Any questions – just ask!"
Mahdi is slightly *embarrassed*. He's not sure what the word "dialogue" really means. He knows the verb "to die" and he also knows that "a log" is a piece of wood. You can put logs on a fire. But "dialogue"? Karl picks up his *biro* and opens his notebook. Pierre laughs again and looks once more at Elke. He knows all about dialogues, especially dialogues with beautiful Swiss women.
Jim Ryan explains enthusiastically:

Übung 5: Lesen Sie weiter und setzen Sie die richtige Verbform ein!

"A dialogue, Mahdi, (1. be) ____________ when two people talk to each other. At the moment I (2. talk) ____________ to you and I (3. try) ____________ to tell you what this word (4. mean) ____________. Now you can tell me that you understand the meaning of the word. OK?"

Mahdi (5. nod) ____________ his head but (6. say) ____________ nothing.

Jim Ryan asks once more.
"Do you understand the meaning of 'dialogue' now?"
Mahdi waves his hands and grins.
"Dialogue," he says. "OK, two people talking to each other – like in the movies." He emphasizes the word "movies".
Karl Schultze carefully writes the word "movies" next to the word "dialogue" and then adds a question mark. He must check this when he goes back to his bed and breakfast *accommodation*.
"Exactly," says Jim Ryan. "But this is not a movie, Mahdi. This is a play. For us the dialogue is in the play. Now, look at your sheets of paper. There are five characters in this short play. I think we can use your real names. The play has got two scenes. The first scene takes place in a small studio, well, a *bedsit* really, and there are two actors, let's say Karl and Franka. Karl is an artist and Franka is his model. Initially, a business relationship, but now they are lovers."
Mahdi and Karl *exchange* glances. This word sounds *suspicious*.
"Karl, however, has a *patroness*. That will be you Elke. You are much older than Karl, and you are a very *jealous* woman."

At this point Elke closes her dictionary, very loudly.
"Jim, Mr Ryan, this is not true. I am not *jealous*. Nobody in Switzerland is *jealous* of other people. Other people are *jealous* of the Swiss. We have got the mountains, the lakes – and the Swiss Franc!"
"Yes, Elke, you're quite right, of course. But don't forget that the Swiss Franc is a very frigid currency. In Britain we think the Swiss Franc is cold and antiseptic. We think that the Swiss are people who show no emotions. Let's see – do you know what the difference between heaven and hell is?"
The students are quiet again and listen *attentively*.
"In hell, the English are the cooks, the Germans are the police, the French are the mechanics, the Swiss are the lovers and the Spanish are the bankers."
Nobody laughs except Mahdi. Elke looks rather miserable. Pierre tries to give moral support with his dark brown eyes. He smoothes back his long black hair and looks very serious. The other two, Karl and Franka, aren't sure if this is a joke. Jim Ryan pauses dramatically.
"In heaven, on the other hand, the English are the police, the Germans are the mechanics, the French are the cooks, the Swiss are the bankers and the Spanish are the lovers. You see, that's the difference between heaven and hell."
Mahdi raises his hand.
"Teacher, Mr Jim Ryan, what about the Omanis?"
Then Franka raises her hand.
"Jim, where are the Irish in this little story?" She smiles sweetly.
Jim Ryan is *impressed*. They understand the story. They understand the humour.
"Well, if you must know... hmmm... the Omanis are the *guardians* of heaven and, well, the Irish must be the *guardians* of hell."

Everybody laughs. They are beginning to relax. Jim Ryan hands out some more sheets.

"Now, the second scene is in a pub – you all know what a pub is, of course."

Karl raises his hand, removes his *glasses* and says very seriously: "A pub, Mr Ryan, is a building where people go to drink and meet their friends. Pubs serve alcoholic and other drinks, and often also food."

"Excellent, Karl," says Jim Ryan, "that's an excellent definition. How do you know that?"

Karl Schultze blushes and then replaces his glasses. He picks up the dictionary.

"It is here, Mr Ryan, in this dictionary." He pronounces the word "dictionary" very slowly, very carefully with an air of triumph. Jim Ryan raises both thumbs in *appreciation*.

"Yes, the dictionary. Have you all got a dictionary?"

Three students look in their *briefcases*. One student grins and does nothing. This, of course, is Pierre Leclerc. He's a Frenchman. Like all Frenchmen he thinks that the English language is really French. You just speak French with an English accent. "Voilà – or, in English 'There you are!' Easy, isn't it?"

"Brilliant," says Jim Ryan. "Pierre, I see that you haven't got a dictionary. Buy one, as soon as possible! You need it! And Karl, remember that we use first names here. My name is Jim, short for James. Now, let's talk about the second scene."

Karl is slightly *upset* and a little *embarrassed*. First you get praise; then you get criticism. These English, they're so unfair! Pierre is angry. His dark brown eyes flash and *send daggers* in the direction of Jim Ryan. Elke *smirks* and Franka claps her hands. Jim, she thinks. Jim Ryan – yes, you are a very *witty*, clever and *handsome* man. Jim carries on.

"Elke and Pierre are sitting in the pub. Elke is passionately in love with Karl, the artist – remember she's older than he is – and she knows that Karl is having an affair with his model Franka. Elke feels *betrayed*. After all, she pays the bills for this artistic genius and wants something more than just paintings in return. She decides that Karl must die. This is a very drastic decision. She will lose the young man she is in love with and the world will lose a potentially great artist. But there we are – jealousy is an uncontrollable passion. She hires Pierre, a professional *hit man*, who shoots Karl in cold blood."

Karl nods his head slowly. He likes the idea. And the more he thinks about it, the more he likes it. He is *involved* with two women in this play. Both are very attractive. He cleans his *glasses* with a special *cloth* and focuses on the redhead from Spain. He is beginning to enjoy this three-week *stay* in Eastcastle, with opportunities that he never thought about before in Gifhorn. Suddenly Mahdi interrupts.

"Jim", he says *shyly*, but with more confidence than before, "Jim, what is my role in the play? I cannot possibly be the barman. I'm a Muslim."

"All very simple, Mahdi. You are an *innocent witness* and you discover the *corpse*."

Mahdi likes the sound of the word "*corpse*". It reminds him of "cops". This is an honourable role in the play. He lowers his head, closes his eyes and puts his hands together. He is very *proud* and accepts his *fate*. He remembers a phrase from the Christian Bible and says, very solemnly:

"Thy will be done, on earth as in heaven."

The others laugh and Jim is happy that the *ice is broken*. Even Elke is *giggling*. Pierre points two fingers and a thumb at Jim Ryan and says, "Bang, bang". Franka looks at Karl, who is making more *notes*. Yes, she thinks, he's rather short and rather *plump* and I hope I don't have to kiss him – but, after all, it is only a play.

Übung 6: Wie lauten die Wörter in der richtigen Reihenfolge?

ÜBUNG 6 !

1. you put can on fire logs a

____

2. picks Karl biro his up

____

3. Franc and the antiseptic cold Swiss is

____

4. pub in meet people friends their a

____

5. Karl die that must decides she

____

6. witness an are innocent you

____

7. broken happy is ice Jim is that the

____

It's Sunday, and there are five days left until the play is performed. Jim and Tracy are down at the harbour, enjoying the sunset. Their affair is now five weeks old. Tracy is throwing a few *pebbles* into the water, wondering how she can turn the conversation to the future – that is, if there is a future for her with Jim Ryan.

"Jim," she smiles. "I want to talk about us. You must know that I'm very much in love with you. What I need to know is where I stand and where you stand in this relationship."

Jim looks out to sea and *shrugs* his shoulders.

"What can I say? You're a wonderful woman, Tracy. You're very attractive, you're great fun and you're *bright*. But – I'm the wrong person for you. My contract finishes next week, the day after the final presentations. And then I'll move on. In fact, I've already got another teaching post. The chance of a lifetime. A five-year contract in the Middle East – tax-free, overseas *allowance* plus marriage and family *allowance* plus..."

Tracy laughs happily.

"Why, Jim, that sounds marvellous. OK, I love Eastcastle, but I've got no real *ties* here. Well, except for the yacht, but I can easily sell that. And I only rent the flat. Where is the contract exactly?"

"If you must know, it's Saudi Arabia, teaching Business English to Saudis in one of the big oil companies. But Tracy, I don't think you quite understand what I'm trying to say."

In her mind, Tracy is already planning how she can *hand in her notice* to the school and her *landlord*. That won't be a problem. In fact, she could leave within a couple of weeks, and she knows that her neighbour is looking for a yacht just like hers. She laughs happily and pulls at Jim's arm.

"Oh, Jim. Don't make things so complicated. I can join you after you move in. Saudi Arabia sounds wonderful. OK, it may be a little hot, but those oil companies provide everything for their employees. And I'm sure I can find some sort of secretarial work. Why are you telling me this only now? It's too good to be true!"

For a few seconds a *cloud* covers the setting sun and the horizon begins to glow pink and red. Jim Ryan turns and stands in front of Tracy. His silhouette casts a long black *shadow* that *envelops* Tracy totally.

"There's something you should know, Tracy. Perhaps you can find it in your heart to forgive me. I'm a married man. I've got two children. The plan is that they join me in Riad in September. Church Hill is just a temporary post. I'm sorry. I'm afraid you and I have no future, none at all."

As the sun reappears, Tracy stands up. Her face says everything. She is shocked. So shocked that she begins to *shiver*, although a warm breeze is blowing off the Channel.

"But the last five weeks – last Thursday – last Monday. Does all that mean nothing? You said that..."

"I know, I know. This is one of my great failings. I'm an impulsive bastard. I always involve *innocent* people. I'm sorry. This, here, is the end for us."

Tracy *scrambles* off the beach towards her car. She is heartbroken. What a fool she is. She loves someone who is already married with two children. The *impostor*! She turns round and screams at Jim Ryan.

"Is this really true!? You flirt with me, you invite me out for drinks and dinner, you make love to me, you even tell me you love me. And all the time you're a married man. Is it true?"

Jim Ryan looks into the distance. Perhaps he feels some shame, because he answers in a very deep voice. But then Jim Ryan is a very good actor.

"Afraid so, Tracy. This is the end of our affair."

Tracy controls herself.

"You know what? You're not an impulsive bastard, Jim Ryan. You are a bastard! A plain and simple bastard. A bastard of the worst kind. Don't ever speak to me again!"

Tracy rushes off to the car, gets in and *roars off*. Jim Ryan kicks a few *pebbles*, puts his hands in his pockets and walks to the nearest pub.

! ÜBUNG 7

Übung 7: Welche der folgenden Aussagen sind wahr? Markieren Sie mit richtig ✔ oder falsch – !

1. Jim and Tracy meet at the harbour early in the morning. ☐
2. Jim thinks Tracy is very stupid. ☐
3. Jim has got a contract in Singapore for five years. ☐
4. Tracy can hand in her notice to her landlord quite quickly. ☐
5. Tracy does not want to move to Saudi Arabia. ☐
6. Jim Ryan has got three children. ☐
7. It is quite warm at the harbour. ☐

Chapter 3: Departure

On Thursday of their third week Class B1 is word perfect in the two scenes of the play. They know the dialogue by heart. They're all enjoying themselves and are now very relaxed in each other's company. Elke really wants to play the part of the older *patroness* and is experimenting with make-up and a couple of *wigs* from the local Amateur Dramatic Society. Pierre is very enthusiastic about his part. As the murderer he must appear totally cool. He must be a professional and show no emotions. This could be difficult for a Frenchman – but, after all, it is only a play. Karl is *over the moon*. He can finally show everyone that under his North German exterior there lies a *tormented* soul, a romantic artist, a man with passion. Franka is now quite happy to be Karl's model. She doesn't have to *take off* her clothes and she doesn't have to kiss Karl. Mahdi goes back to his bed and breakfast every day and thanks Allah that he is simply an *innocent witness*. And he's learning English very fast, which pleases him.

After the *dress rehearsal* the players collect all their papers and *props* and leave for the pub. Jim Ryan stays in the school. He has something important to do.

He knocks at the door of Colonel Lessons's office. He's whistling an old Irish folk song and *feels* totally *at ease*. The "Tracy thing" is over. The B1 class are absolutely marvellous and he knows that the performance on Friday will be a great *success*. The contract for Saudi Arabia is signed and ready to be posted. Of course he's not married! Two children? Why not three, he wonders? But then he comes from Belfast and he isn't Catholic.

"Come in!" shouts Colonel Lessons. Jim Ryan opens the door.

"Ah, Jim. Sit yourself down. Everything OK? Any problems? Would you like a whiskey – it's Irish, you know."

The Colonel reaches up to a *shelf* and takes down a *volume* of the Oxford English Dictionary. He puts it upright on the table, opens one side and takes out a small *hip flask* that is hidden in the *cover*. He smiles broadly. He's dreaming about the South of France and he *suspects* that Jim Ryan wants his salary before the contract finishes. No way! Ryan is a very good teacher but he has to wait four weeks! Jim folds his hands very *modestly*.

"No thanks, Colonel. I still have to do some work on the presentation. Last minute changes."

The Colonel grins. This man is dedicated! He pours himself a large *glass* of whiskey. Perhaps Majorca would be better than Cannes? He looks at Jim and waits.

"Fire away, young man! *Get it off your chest*!"

"Well, Colonel. My contract finishes on Saturday, as you well know." Colonel Lessons *beams* and *nods* his head *encouragingly*.
"The thing is – I need some money, quite a large amount of money, before I take up my next appointment. And I think you can give it to me."

ÜBUNG 8

Übung 8: Setzen Sie die richtigen Präpositionen ein!

1. They know the dialogue ____________ heart.
2. Pierre is very enthusiastic ____________ his part.
3. Karl is ____________ the moon.
4. Jim feels totally ____________ ease.
5. He takes ____________ a small hip flask.
6. Get it ____________ your chest!
7. She takes ____________ her clothes.

A long silence follows. Colonel Lessons takes a *gulp* of whiskey and almost *chokes*. The *impertinence*! The *fellow* really does want payment in advance! These Irish are so *cocky*!
"I'm not quite sure what you're getting at, Ryan."
Jim *settles back* in the chair and takes out a notebook.
"Colonel, just listen to the *notes* I have here. You charge £800 per student for a course of three weeks. You pay the teacher £600 pounds for three weeks. You get a 20% *cut* from the bed and breakfast *accommodation*. You pick up 10% from the two pubs where the students drink. You give the students Mickey Mouse certificates for completing the course. You aren't even registered with any of

the agencies that control courses for teaching English as a foreign language. In fact, Church Hill School for English is a gold mine and, at the moment, all the gold goes to you."

The Colonel is as *white as a sheet*. He takes another *gulp* of whiskey. Jim Ryan stands up and sweeps his arm around the room.

"This building isn't *fireproof*. There are no escape routes from upstairs. You even illegally employ Polish migrants to do the repairs. All in all, you are making a great deal of money *under false pretences*."

The Colonel finishes his whiskey and pours another. His voice is now very loud.

"This is *blackmail*, Ryan! Everything you say may be true. But – and it's a big but – it may NOT be true. Now, you're a man of business. What do you really want?"

Jim Ryan is calm and cool.

"Colonel, I can report all of this tomorrow to the Ministry of Education or the Department of Health and Safety. Then you're ruined. Am I right – or, am I right?"

There is a long pause as the Colonel thinks. He sees Majorca sinking, the South of France disappearing in a *mist*.

"How much?"

Jim Ryan grins, sits down and crosses his legs. He puts the notebook into his pocket.

"30 *grand*, Colonel. And that's a *bargain*. I leave for Saudi Arabia on Sunday. Give me the money at the station and then everything's OK."

The Colonel waits for a moment, working out the price of *property* between Cannes and Calais.

"20," he says, in a very military tone. Ryan smiles.

"OK, let's make it 25. Sunday, at the station, used *notes* in a brown envelope."

Jim Ryan stands up and holds out his hand. Colonel Lessons shakes it *vigorously*.
"You're a bastard, Ryan. Now get out!"
After Jim Ryan leaves the office, Lessons dials Tracy's number.
"Tracy! We need some cash, fairly quickly. I'll give you the details tomorrow but we're talking about 25,000. That's possible, isn't it?"
"Of course, Colonel. What's wrong?"
Colonel Lessons tries to pour another whisky but the *hip flask* is now empty.
"Nothing, Tracy. Nothing at all. We'll sort it out tomorrow. Just take the money out of the bank and keep it in your flat till Sunday."

ÜBUNG 9 !

Übung 9: Welche Wörter haben eine ähnliche Bedeutung? Ordnen Sie zu!

1. cocky	☐ energetically
2. cut	☐ relaxed
3. issue	☐ impertinent
4. under false pretences	☐ thousand
5. calm	☐ commission
6. grand	☐ distribute
7. vigorously	☐ illegally

Friday is the day of the presentations. The four groups are ready and waiting. Janet's group starts at 10 in the morning. They sing traditional songs like "Greensleeves", but also have a Karaoke session. Pat's group organizes various activities in the back garden: a traditional English Fête – the *sack race* is a tremendous *success*. The third group, with Terry *in charge*, produces a midday meal. The students can choose from *bangers and mash, toad-in-the-hole* or *shepherd's pie*. They can also drink "Real Ale", traditional English beer. This item on the menu, however, is not very popular, particularly with the Japanese students. At 3 p.m. it's the turn of Jim Ryan's group. Everybody goes into the main hall, a large room with a stage at the back. Here they all sit down in a sort of circle. The students are laughing and chattering, some in their own language, but most of them are talking in English. They're very pleased with their progress and are *looking forward to* the final presentation. Jim, Elke, Franka, Karl, Mahdi and Pierre walk to the front and disappear behind a large curtain. Karl steps out and addresses the audience.

"Ladies and gentlemen, it is our pleasure to present a short play. Look, please, at your programme. You all know the motto of Church Hill School, namely 'Learning by Doing', but the title of our play is 'Learning by Killing'. This is an example of English irony."

The students *chuckle* and begin to clap. Karl is *sweating* but very happy that his joke is appreciated. He continues.

"The plot is simple. Love, *betrayal*, jealousy and murder. I hope that you enjoy our little play. The text, by the way, is included in your programme."

Karl *bows* rather *awkwardly*, holding his *glasses*, and then rushes backstage. The curtain is drawn back. The students smile and begin to clap again. Jim Ryan and his team have created an authentic flat with *props*. Most students recognize the sort of *bedsit* that they live in. They see a bed, a table, two chairs, a wash basin but also *canvasses* and half-finished paintings.

The first scene, relatively short, is performed. Karl and Franka are very *convincing*. All the students can appreciate that passion plays an important role in this little play.

They now know that something "dramatic" will happen in the second scene. After the curtain is opened again, there is even more applause. This time the *setting* is a pub. It looks just like the "The Cherry Tree", the pub where most of the students spend their evenings. It's only two hundred metres from the school. Of course, they don't know that Colonel Lessons has "an arrangement" with the *landlord*. 10%!

There are several comfortable chairs and a table as the bar, with pieces painted to look like dark, Victorian wood. Lots of *glasses* hanging upside down and bottles behind, also upside down. Music is playing quietly in the background. Elke and Pierre are sitting at a table, whispering. The students study the text in the programme, occasionally looking at the actors.

E: So, Pierre, you know what to do. Have you got the gun?

P: Do you want to see it? I can show it to you.

E: Not here, you fool. People may be looking at us. You know the plan. I have an argument with Karl. A lovers' *tiff*, as they say. I tell him that I know he is having an affair – an affair with that silly young woman, Franka. I leave and go to the car-park. He follows me. I know he will. He wants my money and my contacts. I drive away and then you shoot. It's all a great tragedy and the world will lose a great artist. But there is no other solution. Franka will survive and I will survive. There are other Karls on this planet and Art, too, will survive. Think of... Aaah, here he comes!

Pierre moves to another table as Karl enters the pub. Karl apologizes for being late and sits in a chair. Then he tells Elke all about Franka, how pretty she is, much prettier than his previous model. The audience smile and *chuckle*. Dramatic Irony. They already know much more about what is happening than Karl does. Then

Karl says that he wants to give his new painting the title "Temptation". There is a long pause and then something *snaps* in Elke. She takes out a mirror and looks at her *wrinkles*.

E: Oh, sweet bird of youth! And I am so old and wrinkled and tired. I have nothing to offer anymore.

K: Now, Elke. You know that that's simply not true. You're the most beautiful woman in the world. You are my muse, you are my inspiration, my sun and my moon – and you are also the love of my life!

The audience cannot help laughing. After all, Elke, despite her make-up, is a very attractive woman and Karl – well, Karl is rather short and *plump*. And he wears *glasses*. Elke continues.

E: Thank you, Karl. But that's not enough. I may be the love of your life but you don't really love ME! You only love my money! You're only interested in me because I pay your bills! Listen, I know, I know everything! I know what's going on. I know you are having an affair with this woman, this girl. So we must end our affairs, both of them. The sexual affair... and the business affair!

Übung 10: Setzen Sie die Verben in der richtigen Form (Present Simple oder Present Progressive) ein!

K: Don't say that Elke! How can you? I love you more than words can say. I (1. think) ______________________ of you every minute of the day. Please don't say we're finished.

E: But we are, my dearest. You know that I am a very possessive woman. Goodbye!

Elke (2. leave) ________________. Karl, *stunned*, sits for a moment longer and then (3. rush) ________________ out. Pierre (4. hurry) ________________ to the door and (5. follow) ________________ him. A shot is heard in the background as a car drives away. Suddenly Mahdi appears.

M: Help! Someone help! Call the police. Call an ambulance. A man (6. lie) ________________ in the car park! I think he (7. die) ________________. Quickly!

Mahdi exits and returns a few moments later. He raises his hands and addresses the audience.

M: The man is dead. This is a terrible tragedy. His last words were “Elke, Franka, temptation”. May he *rest in peace*.

The curtain is drawn and the students of Church Hill School begin to applaud. Colonel Lessons appears from the front of the hall, marches to the stage and then turns to the audience, leading them in their *appreciation*. They clap their hands, louder and louder. What a superb end to three weeks in Eastcastle. All the presentations. Food, songs, village life! The players step round the curtain, holding hands. Elke *bows* first and the others follow. They are all smiling, pleased that the production is so *successful*. Karl polishes his *glasses*, raises his arms in triumph and then waves his hands to silence the audience. He's absolutely *thrilled*.

"Ladies and gentlemen. Thank you for your *appreciation*. You *obviously* liked our little play. Now we must give thanks to our teacher, director and producer – Jim Ryan!! Jim, please come out!"

The students continue to clap – and clap – and clap. Nobody appears. Karl whispers to Mahdi, who then disappears behind the curtain. The clap becomes a slow handclap. Everybody is waiting for Jim Ryan. Suddenly Mahdi rushes through the curtain, pulling it down and *knocking over* several of the *props*. He's *frantic*. He turns to the players and then to the audience. He raises his hands and begins to cry. The students begin to sit down. Is this part of the play, they wonder? Mahdi turns to Pierre and whispers something. Pierre marches forward. He looks at the audience grimly.

"Something is very wrong here. Sacre-bleu! Jim Ryan is dead. Please leave the room. This is not a play. Jim Ryan, our teacher, is dead!"

The curtain closes again. Some of the younger students begin to scream.

Übung 11: Übersetzen Sie folgende Sätze ins Deutsche!

ÜBUNG 11 !

1. They are ready to present their tasks.

____

2. The students are laughing and chattering.

____

3. They are looking forward to the presentation.

____

4. Mahdi disappears behind the curtain.

5. I drive away and then you shoot.

6. Karl polishes his glasses.

7. Some students begin to scream.

Chapter 4: Left Luggage

Inspector Watson from the local police is tired. It's Saturday morning and the temperature is already around 30 degrees. But he must continue with the interviews. Most of the students want to leave on Sunday. The five members of Jim Ryan's class are extremely *upset* and can give no useful information. The revolver from the play is on the *desk* in front of him. It's plastic, of course, and cannot be used to kill anyone. Pierre still has the *receipt* from the local toyshop – £5.50. Watson also has the first report from forensic. This says that the murderer must have shot Ryan from a corner behind the stage, probably the left-hand corner, because that's where the door to the back garden is. The murderer must be *familiar with* guns and is also a very good *marksman*. After all, the distance from the door to Ryan's body is about 10 metres. The next student, a young man from Terry's class, knocks and enters the room.

"Ah, let's see." Watson looks at his list. "You must be Mr Olsen, from Denmark I think."

"That's right, Inspector. How can I help?"
"Well, according to my plan here, your seat was in the second row, the last one on the right-hand side, so perhaps you could actually see this door which leads into the garden?"
Jens Olsen smiles and says:

Übung 12: Setzen Sie die Verben in der Past Simple Form ein!

ÜBUNG 12 !

"I understand, Inspector. Now let me think back." He concentrates. "The play (1. be) ______________ great fun. The actors (2. be) ______________ superb. Very good English. We (3. understand) __________________________ everything. After Elke (4. leave) ________________ the pub, the audience were all very quiet. We (5. know) _______________ that something was going to happen, a fight or a murder. When the gun *went off*, there was some laughter – we all knew it was a toy gun. And I can tell you this. After the shot, I (6. hear) ____________________ three sounds very clearly. One was a cry of pain. Well, we (7. think) ____________________ that was part of the play."

"Go on," says Inspector Watson softly.
"The second was a *thud* – is that what you say in English?" Watson looks up from his notebook and *nods*.
"It was like a body that falls to the ground. Or the floor. The main hall has wooden floorboards. And then, in the total silence before the applause, someone *slammed* a door. It must be this door on

your plan. So the killer left the main hall by this door – is that what you think?"

"Thank you, Mr Olsen. Very helpful. When do you return to Denmark?"

"Monday, Inspector. From Heathrow to Kastrup, that's the airport in Copenhagen."

After Jens Olsen leaves the room, Watson leans back in his chair. So! His hypothesis is correct. The killer shot from behind and exited into the garden. But who is the killer? And where is the weapon? And what is the motive? Questions, questions – and no answers!

The interviews continue. After the students, the teachers – and then, finally, the *staff*. Rose can give no helpful information. She was there at the performance but saw and heard nothing *strange*. Tracy was at home. She always has Friday afternoons free. The last person to come in is Mrs Bradley, the cleaner. Inspector Watson begins to feel that this *case* may remain *unsolved*. It could be "the perfect murder".

"Sit down, Mrs Bradley. Now, I wonder if you can tell me why someone wanted to kill Jim Ryan?"

"Well, Inspector, I'm not really sure. I mean, perhaps it's nothing important – but on Thursday evening, when I started to *mop* the floor..."

! ÜBUNG 13

Übung 13: Beantworten Sie folgende Fragen auf Englisch!

1. Why can Ryan's class give no useful information?

____

2. How much did the toy gun cost?

____

3. Where was Olsen's seat?

4. How many sounds did Olsen hear?

5. Where was Tracy on Friday?

6. What is the cleaner's name?

7. Where does Olsen live?

While Inspector Watson is doing his interviews, Colonel Lessons is at Number 19. He's happy that he doesn't need to be at Church Hill until the late afternoon. Tracy is organizing everything and Rose is there, too. He orders another gin and tonic and smiles at the barmaid. Well, he thinks, that's all over. Jim Ryan's dead. No *investigations* from the Ministry of Education. OK, those students from the B1 class are rather *upset* and one or two others may miss their flights back home. Perhaps I'll give them a rebate – say £50 – and then everything will be forgotten. An unfortunate *incident*. Very unfortunate for Jim Ryan! The Colonel, a military man through and through, turns to the collection of antique guns behind the bar.

"Judy, tell me. That collection behind you. Do all those guns still work?"

The barmaid *shrugs* her shoulders and pours another pint of beer.

"Colonel, to be honest, I've no idea. They belong to the Secretary of the Golf Club. He's a collector, you know. But why don't you ask Tracy Dean. She was the barmaid here before me. She'll know. Another gin and tonic, Colonel?"

"Only if you *twist my arm*, Judy! Yes, of course! Why not? I'm feeling lucky today!"

As the Colonel is *sipping* his gin and tonic the phone rings. Judy picks it up. After a few seconds she turns to Lessons and whispers loudly.

"It's the police, Colonel. An Inspector Watson. He wants to see you down at the school – immediately!"

"Damn!" says Lessons. "OK, Judy, tell him I'm on my way."

The Colonel gulps the rest of his drink and heads out to the Rolls Royce.

Inspector Watson is now very confident that he can *solve* the murder. He *loosens his collar*. When Colonel Lessons comes in, he writes the time in his notebook: 15:34.

"Colonel, how good of you to come so quickly. No problems, I hope."

The Colonel is extremely angry.

"Now, listen Watson. This is a murder *case*, *obviously*. And I want you to find the murderer. I can't *afford* to have this sort of scandal hanging over Church Hill!"

Watson looks out to the garden and then *stares* at Colonel Lessons.

"But you can *afford* to take out £25,000 from your bank– one day before Jim Ryan is murdered. I wonder if there's a connection?"

Lessons is *flabbergasted*.

"Now, look here, Inspector! I don't think you realize how much my school pays in local taxes. Without this school, Eastcastle is nothing. And how do you know about the £25,000, anyway?"

"Have you got a cleaning lady, Colonel?"

Lessons sits down. What on earth is this little man, Watson from the local police, trying to say?
"Of course we've got *staff*," shouts the Colonel. "Ask my daughter, Rose. She's *in charge of* all that."
Watson deals his trump card.
"Yes, I know. And I also now know that your cleaner's name is Mrs Bradley. She comes in every weekday around six. Now, where were you Colonel, between six and seven on Thursday? Not at the Golf Club, so they tell me."
Lessons begins to *splutter*. He knows exactly where he was – in his office with that bastard Jim Ryan.
"Er – wait a second, Inspector. Let's see – Thursday. Back from the clubhouse around four to check up on *accounts*. Last-minute preparations for Friday, you know, *fire precautions* and so on. Ah, yes! A short talk with Jim Ryan about his references. He wants – sorry, he wanted to take up a post in Saudi Arabia. Well, there were no problems. He was an excellent member of *staff* here during his six-week *stay*. Then down to the Pig and Whistle for dinner. Yes, that's it. Thursday. Oh, and a phone call to Tracy to withdraw the £25,000. And, dear Inspector Watson, I need that money to pay for certain repairs to the roof and so on. Cash payments, you know. Cash, Inspector – no tax, no insurance. I think you call it '*moonlighting*'."
Inspector Watson *sighs* and looks at the ceiling.
"A good story, Colonel. It sounds very *convincing*. But Mrs Bradley tells me a very different story. She's cleaning the floor outside your office and hears a loud argument between you and Ryan. Now, she isn't an *eavesdropper*, but she hears a reference to the Ministry of Education and the word '*blackmail*' – and the sum of £25,000. After a few minutes Ryan comes out, whistling *cheerfully*. Then, around seven, you come out. You are so angry that

you don't even say goodbye. *By the way*, I also know that you have several prizes for being an excellent *marksman* with a pistol. I'm afraid, Colonel, that I must ask you to come down to the police station."

Watson stands up and calls in the constable waiting outside. The Colonel laughs, slightly hysterically. For some reason, he sees the sun setting on Majorca and the South of France, yet again. Even on Calais.

! ÜBUNG 14

Übung 14: Formulieren Sie folgende Sätze als Fragen!

1. Watson is doing his interviews.

___

2. They order another gin.

___

3. He turns to the gun collection.

___

4. He laughs hysterically.

___

5. His school pays local taxes.

___

6. She's cleaning the floor.

___

7. The sun is setting on Eastcastle.

"You've got this all wrong, Inspector. I'm totally *innocent...*" But he has no time to explain. The constable puts on the *handcuffs* and leads him out to the police car. The Colonel sees his gleaming Roller in the *drive*. This time it will be a police cell – not Number 19.

Watson is relieved. He congratulates himself. Excellent detective work, he thinks. I may get *promotion* for solving this *case* so quickly. He *gathers* his *notes*, walks to his car and then decides to have a good pint of bitter in his local pub. Church Hill School, the old Victorian *mansion*, is now empty. The *mellowed brickwork* reflects the sun as Watson *slams* the front door shut.

About two miles out from the harbour, Tracy, on her yacht, is gliding through the waves of the English Channel. She looks towards the town and admires the ancient castle standing at the top of the cliffs. She doesn't feel sorry for the Colonel. He's a pompous bastard anyway. Only Tracy knows who really killed Jim Ryan. She gently hums the sea shanty about Billy Boy and Nancy Grey. She thinks about the £25,000 in a brown envelope and her flight to New York on Monday. Then she suddenly turns and throws the revolver into the water.

MURDER IN ROSEMEADOWS

Anne Ellsworth

Chapter 1: What Margie Said to Her Friend

At nine o'clock, Edith becomes restless. Where is Margie? That afternoon her friend said she would come over at seven in the evening. Now it is two hours later, and still there is no sign of Margie.

"I've got to go over to Margie's house and see if everything is all right," she says.

Her husband Ted looks up from the television. "It's *foggy* outside," he says. "You shouldn't go out by yourself."

"But I have a *strange* feeling about her," Margie insists. "She was acting funny this afternoon when I visited her at the bookshop. She said she had to tell me something. When I asked her what it was, she said, 'Not here. Later! I'll come over this evening.'"

"Well, maybe she just forgot," Ted responds with a shrug and turns back to the rugby game on television.

Edith *sighs*. She cannot believe that Margie would forget to come over this evening. Margie was so nervous this afternoon. What else did she say? Oh yes...

ÜBUNG 1

Übung 1: Setzen Sie die Verben ins Simple Past!

1. Margie insists: ____________________
2. she is acting: ____________________
3. Edith sighs: ____________________

4. she cannot believe: ____________________

5. Margie forgets: ____________________

6. she says: ____________________

Luckily there is a *commercial break* on television.
"She also said something *strange*, Ted. She said, 'It had to be Ashley.' And then she pointed at a book next to the *cash register*. When I asked her what this was all about, she looked at me as if she was afraid of something – or someone. And she just shook her head and told me to be quiet. She said she'd come over this evening at seven."
Her husband *nods* as he picks up his glass of ale. "That does sound *strange*. What book was she pointing at?"
Edith is thinking hard. It was some book about murders, wasn't it? Then she remembers. "It was called 'The Greatest *Unsolved* Murder Mysteries'. It's one of the books from her *library*. I myself never read it, but..."
Ted looks at her and gets up from his chair. "You're right, that IS *strange*. Let's drive over there and make sure nothing has happened to her."
He turns off the television. Oh well, doesn't matter, he *sigh*s. His team is losing the game anyway.

The *fog* is so thick that Ted almost misses the small *cottage* where Margaret Prim lives by herself. The words "Tearose *Cottage*" over the front door tell of Margie's love for roses, and so does her front garden. There are roses in big pots and roses in pretty *baskets* on her doorstep. Roses in boxes sit on her *window sills*, and roses grow out of an old wooden *barrel* next to the low white iron gate. A tall climbing rose reaches up to the roof, and *hedge* roses grow along the narrow path from the gate to the door.

"Ouch!" Ted cries out when he scratches his hand on one of the *hedge* roses.

"Those damn roses are all over the place," he *curses* while rubbing the back of his hand. "I say this one *pounced on* me!"

"No, it didn't!" Edith smiles and shakes her head. "Margie just loves roses, that's all. And they are lovely, aren't they? Hers still *blossom* in November. I wonder how she does it?"

But her husband does not care about blossoming roses in November. He walks carefully past a large rose pot on the doorstep and rings the doorbell.

There is no answer.

Again he presses the doorbell.

Again everything remains silent.

"She doesn't seem to be home," he says to Edith.

"But where would she be at this time in the evening?" Edith wonders. "Perhaps she just didn't hear the bell."

She knocks on the door. "Margie! Are you there?"

No sign of Margie.

Ted turns the *doorknob*. The door opens.

"That's *strange*," Edith remarks. "She always locks her front door when she leaves the house."

They enter the long hallway. "Margie! Hello? Are you there?"

Margie does not answer. But now they hear voices. And music.

"Do you hear that?" Edith asks.

Ted *nods*. "It's coming from the sitting room."

"It sounds like television," Edith says. "Then Margie must be home after all!"

"Perhaps she just fell asleep," Ted says. "Tonight's programme can do that to you – if you don't like rugby, of course."

They walk past the rose pictures in pastel *frames* that hang in the hallway. Then they reach the sitting room. The door is open.

“Hello, Margie? It’s us – Edith and Ted!” Edith calls out softly because she does not want to frighten her friend.

Übung 2: Lesen Sie weiter und setzen Sie folgende Substantive ein! ***(blossoms, ground, sofa, moments, flowers, room, garden, glasses, wallpaper)***

Ted follows her into the sitting room. He hasn’t been to Margie’s home in a while. For a few (1.) ____________________ he is blinded by the wallpaper. Margie must have redecorated her sitting (2.) ______________________________. Now it is one great big rose (3.) ____________________ with pink rose (4.) ____________________ and yellow *canaries* everywhere.

“Isn’t that (5.) _________________________ pretty?” Edith whispers. “Margie put it up herself in summer. She’s so *proud* of it!”

“Very pretty, yes. But don’t you think it’s a bit too much?” He *blinks* a few times until he can see past the (6.) _______________ and the birds. Then he points at the sofa. “There she is. She’s sleeping.”

Edith’s friend is lying on the (7.) _________________. The *remote control* is sitting on the coffee table and her *glasses* have fallen to the (8.) ____________________.

“She must have taken her (9.) _________________ off and gone to sleep,” Margie whispers.

"No wonder – *considering* what she was watching," Ted says and points at the television. "Four hours of 'War and Peace'. Didn't they just show it the other week?"

"No, that was last month, dear," Edith answers. "And anyway, she wanted to come over to see me, remember?"

She walks over to the sofa and touches Margie's arm. "Margie, wake up! We're here! Edith and Ted."

However, the woman on the sofa does not wake up. "Margie! Wake up, will you?" Now Edith shakes her friend softly. Margie's head *lolls* to the side.

Edith turns round to Ted, who is standing behind her. She looks at him with wide eyes. "Ted, I think there's something wrong with her."

He bends down and *grabs* Margie's *wrist*. After a few seconds he lets go of her arm and turns round.

"Darling," he says slowly. "She's not sleeping. She's dead."

Edith is too shocked to cry. She turns *pale* and sinks into the armchair.

"Darling, are you alright?" Ted asks *worried*. He walks over to her and holds her tight.

"How – how can she be dead?" Edith *stares* at him. "After all, I spoke to her just this afternoon!"

"She must have had a heart attack," Ted says. "Didn't she say recently that she was having heart problems?"

Edith *nods*. "You're right. She had to get heart medicine last month. Poor Margie. Poor, poor Margie." *Tenderly* she runs her hand over the small *cushion* on the chair. It has the same rose-*canary* pattern as the wallpaper.

"Margie was so happy about this lovely pattern," she says. "It took her months to find it."

Now she starts to cry.

"We've got to call Doc Baker," her husband says softly. "He'll know what to do."

Doc Baker is the only doctor in the village. He is called whenever someone in Rosemeadows is born or dies, has *measles*, a broken arm, the flu or a toothache. He is also called whenever someone in Rosemeadows celebrates a birthday, gets married or simply feels lonely.

Übung 3: Ordnen Sie die Beschreibungen den folgenden Krankheiten zu!

(a toothache, a broken arm, measles, the flu, seasickness, a headache)

1. You have red spots all over your body. ______________
2. It feels like hammering inside your head. ______________
3. You can't use your hand. ______________
4. Your whole mouth hurts. ______________
5. You feel hot, cold and tired at the same time. ______________
6. You don't feel well on a boat. ______________

The good doctor also gets invited to a lot of suppers.

Everyone loves Doc Baker. And Doc Baker loves his job. He knows every family, every *widow*, every child and every dog in Rosemeadows.

He also knows every cat in the village.

"*By the way*, where is Margaret's *tomcat*?" the doctor asks after he has come over to examine Margie and has *pronounced* her *dead*.

"What's his name again? Ah yes – Major Tom. Have you seen him?"
Ted shakes his head. "No, I forgot all about him. Edith, did you see Margie's cat anywhere when we entered the house?"
Edith raises her head and *stares* at the men. "No, actually I haven't. That's *strange*. Margie always feeds him in the evening and only lets him out into the garden when she gets ready for bed. He should be somewhere in the house. Perhaps he is so shocked about Margie's death that he's hiding somewhere. Cats sense when something is wrong. Are you sure it was a heart attack?"
The doctor *nods* thoughtfully. "It looks like an acute heart attack. After all, Margaret *complained* about an irregular heartbeat, and I gave her heart medication last month."
Ted leaves the sitting room to look for the cat. After all, the poor animal must not be left behind if it is still somewhere in the house. He would *starve to death*.
Then Edith remembers how nervous Margie was this afternoon. She gets up and walks over to the television set where "War and Peace" has finally come to its tragic end. "Could something she was worrying about give her a heart attack?" she asks as she turns it off.
Baker looks at her curiously. "It's possible. Why – was she *worried* about something? Did she tell you what it was?"
Edith shakes her head. "No, but she wanted to tell me tonight." Then she tells Doc Baker what Margie said to her at the bookshop that afternoon.
"'It had to be Ashley'? 'Greatest *Unsolved* Murder Mysteries'?" the doctor repeats *baffled*. "That sounds quite mysterious! Do you know who she was talking about? Did she know this Ashley? Could it be a book character? Or a friend from her past? After all, no one by that name lives in Rosemeadows."

Übung 4: Setzen Sie folgende Verben in die Lücken ein!
(presses, look at, talked, walks, think, looking for, take, going, calling, wake up)

ÜBUNG 4 !

She (1.) ____________________ back to the armchair deep in thought. "I have no idea," she says. She is *cradling* the small, soft *cushion* as if it was a baby. Or Margie. She still cannot *bear* to (2.) ________________ her dead friend on the sofa. She simply can't believe she is dead. Perhaps this is all a very bad dream, and she will (3.) ________________ in a moment. "You know that her husband's name was Wilbur. She never (4.) ________________ about any Ashleys to me. And I don't (5.) ________________ she was keeping any secrets from me. After all, I was her best friend. We told each other everything, really. Oh dear, I am going to miss her so much."

She hears Ted (6.) ____________________ softly, "Major Tom, where are you? Come, kitty kitty!" She feels the tears *well up* in her eyes again and (7.) ________________ her face into the *cheerful* pink and yellow *cushion*.

"Oh Margie," she cries bitterly. "What am I (8.) ________________ to do without you?"

Doc Baker is already (9.) ________________ the small bottle he always keeps in his bag for *cases* like these. It is a very effective medicine for *soothing* a broken heart. Though he almost feels that he should (10.) __________________ some too.

"I think everyone is going to miss her very much, Edith."
Ted steps into the small room where Margie stored potatoes, apples, jellies and jams, vegetables and fruit from her garden *pre-served* in glass jars and her wonderful homemade peach brandy. Typically for Margie, even in this little room everything is arranged very *neatly.* Dreaming of her delicious jams that he has enjoyed on his toast for breakfast so many times, he almost *stumbles* over a soft little black doormat. But it isn't a doormat after all.
It is Major Tom. He is stretched out on the stone floor, sleeping peacefully.
"Ah, here you are," Ted says and kneels down to *stroke* the cat. "Wake up, sleepy head! I have bad news for you – your mummy is gone, and I *bet* Edith will make me take you home with us."
Major Tom does not even wake up when Ted begins to *stroke* him. Now Ted notices that the cat's eyes are wide open, but he is not moving at all.
He isn't even breathing.
"Oh my God," Ted says. He gets up in a hurry and runs down the hallway, shouting "He's dead! The cat is dead, too! There's got to be something wrong here – Major Tom is dead!"

Chapter 2: A Poisoned Lamb Stew

Constable Harold Flynn *grabs* the last piece of the pizza he was eating when the phone rang. He does not *bother* to put on his police uniform. There is no time for that. Doc Baker just reported Margaret Prim's death and *suspects* that she *died of unnatural causes*.

A murder in Rosemeadows? Flynn thinks to himself as he picks up his jacket with his free hand. He hurries to the *patrol car* sitting in his *driveway* and *stuffs* the rest of the pizza into his mouth. A real murder? That's hard to *swallow*!

He *swallow*s the last bite of the pizza and drives over to the house as fast as the thick *fog* allows.

Soft golden light shines through the windows in the small *cottage*. Rose bushes *cheerfully* welcome the constable as if this was just another supper *invitation* from the *widow* Margaret Prim.

But it is not. There will never be another one of her delicious *pot roasts* or *lamb stew*s waiting for him in the oven. How many *cosy* evenings has he spent here in the company of Margaret and her homemade peach brandy! Sometimes Betty, his loyal assistant, came as well. Then they had a *hearty* supper, a game of Scrabble and lots of *hearty* laughter, because none of them really knew the rules of the game. They made up the silliest words, and everyone was a winner.

Margaret always called Betty Bette, because her last name is Davis. And she always called him Errol. Just like that old American actor, Errol Flynn.

Übung 5: Unterstreichen Sie das „schwarze Schaf"!

ÜBUNG 5 !

1. beer, brandy, juice, wine
2. cottage, window, house, church
3. roast, supper, stew, pizza
4. singer, actor, widow, musician
5. potatoes, jams, apples, peaches
6. swallow, soothe, stuff, eat
7. wake up, feel, sleep, eyes

8. fast, delicious, shine, golden
9. patrol car, driveway, police uniform, constable

He smiles sadly and walks up the garden path. A *branch* of one of the roses along the path *clings to* his trousers as if wanting to stop him from going to the front door. Even though he never *admitted* it, he kind of likes the nickname everyone in the village calls him by. Errol Flynn. It does sound classy.

He finds the doctor with the Pearsons in the kitchen. Edith Pearson is in tears. She is pressing a small *cushion* to her *bosom* and crying, "Poor Margie... poor Major Tom... oh, my God, what a terrible, terrible thing..."

Doc Baker is glad when the police officer enters the kitchen. "Thank God you're here, Errol – I mean Harold. There's something *fishy* about Margaret's death. They're both dead – her and her cat." Then he and Ted tell Flynn everything they know, while Edith slowly *calms down*.

"Tonight's supper is still here in the pot," Ted says, opening the oven door. "You see? She had stew – and the cat must have had some, too. There is still some stew left over in his cat dish."

"That's *strange*," Flynn says. Suddenly the thought of the many times when he ate Margaret's delicious stew makes him feel *queasy*. Could the stew be *poisoned*? He opens the lid and *sniffs* at the soup. It has a faint smell of *almonds*. "There could be cyanide in here. I will ask the lab to test the stew for *poisons*."

Finally Edith has herself enough under control to tell the constable about her visit to Margaret's bookshop this afternoon.

"'It had to be Ashley'?" Flynn is *baffled*. "Who is Ashley? And this book she pointed at – are you sure it was called 'The Greatest *Unsolved* Murder Mysteries'?"

"Of course I'm sure. It it one of the books from her *library*. The

summer tourists *borrowed* it all the time. I never read it, but I think Margie did. Yes – she once told me that there are a lot of interesting *unsolved* murder *cases* in it."
Flynn writes down the title of the book. He will put Betty to work on this. She simply loves murder mysteries.
But somehow he does not think she will love THIS murder mystery – the murder of Margaret Prim.
The report from the laboratory is on Flynn's *desk* two days later.
"Have you seen the test results?" Betty asks him in the morning when he walks in. He hasn't even had time yet to *take off* his jacket.
"No, but I'm sure you have," the constable replies and smiles to himself. He has never seen his secretary as highly motivated as since this murder happened. Her cheeks are rosy, her eyes are *bright*, and she is *determined* to *solve* this murder *case*.
If necessary, by herself.

Übung 6: Lesen Sie weiter und unterstreichen Sie die richtigen Präpositionen!

"Yes, I did take a quick look (1.) at/on it," Betty *admits*. Flynn is certain that she read the whole report (2.) by/from beginning to end. "And there was enough cyanide (3.) in/into the stew to kill a horse or two!"
Somehow this does not surprise Flynn very much. A woman AND her cat die (4.) after/before eating the same food? That cannot mean anything but *poison*! The only thing that does surprise him a bit is the high concentration (5.) of/from the *poison* in the stew.
"Seems that the murderer doesn't know very much (6.) over/about *poison*," he says. "He – or she – wanted to make one hundred percent sure that Margaret would not *survive* her last supper."

Betty's cheeks turn even more rosy, and her eyes glitter. "That's exactly what I was thinking myself! It can't have been a doctor, can it? Or a pharmacist. He or she would know how little cyanide is needed to kill a human."

"Unless that is what the murderer wants us to think," Flynn says.

"Oh, how smart you are!" Betty cries excitedly. "That's true! What if it WAS a doctor? What if it was Doc Baker himself?"

Then she shakes her head. "How silly of me! If he *poisoned* her, then why would he ask about her cat and call you? He would just say that she *died of natural causes* – such as a heart attack."

"And what reason would he have for killing her, anyhow?" Flynn points out.

"You're right. No doctor. But perhaps a man named Ashley?"

"Yes, I think if we find this Ashley, we may have our murderer," Harold Flynn says slowly. "Let's go over to her shop and look for the book and *clue*s that may lead us to this mysterious Ashley. Did Margaret ever *mention* any Ashley to you? Perhaps an old boyfriend before she met Wilbur? An old friend from her youth?"

Thinking hard, Betty buttons up her coat. "Not that I can remember. And the only Ashley I know is the one in the *novel* '*Gone With The Wind*'."

"Well, it can't be that Ashley," Flynn remarks. "That one really HAS gone with the wind..."

Margaret Prim's bookshop is located in the centre of Rosemeadows. The name of the shop, "Margie's *Treasure Chest*", is written on the large front window. Her latest book treasures are laid out in the window. It is a collection of international cookbooks, lovingly decorated with red apples, green bottles filled with her peach brandy and golden autumn leaves. And of course a few dried rose *blossoms* are *scattered* here and there as well.

“Show me your window and I’ll tell you who you are,” Betty remarks. “You can tell that Margie loved to cook, loved roses and loved pretty decorations, can’t you?”
Flynn *swallows* the *lump* in his *throat* that almost turns into tears. “Well, I suppose you can,” he says in a *gruff* voice. That is because he really liked the *cheerful* and funny *widow*. But now he has work to do, and even though he loves his job, he does not like it now. Not today. Not when it means the murder of Margie Prim.
He likes it even less when he turns the shop key in the lock, opens the door and steps inside.

Übung 7: Bringen Sie die Wörter in die richtige Reihenfolge!

ÜBUNG 7 !

1. me your window show

____

2. swallows Flynn the throat his in lump

____

3. key the shop he lock the in turns

____

4. window on front the the is name written

____

5. our have we may murderer

____

6. shop let’s over her to go

____

"Oh no," he says to Betty, who is still looking at the window from the outside. "Take a look at this, will you?"

Betty enters the shop behind him. "Dear God!" she exclaims. "What chaos!"

She looks around with wide eyes. All the books have been taken from their *shelves* and are *scattered* on the floor. A large box has been *turned over* and is lying in the centre of the shop. All the books that were in the box are in a *pile* on the ground. Even the *cash register* is lying on its side. "Somebody must have broken into the shop," she says shocked.

"And I have a good idea who THAT was," Flynn says angrily. "It had to be Ashley."

Three hours later it is clear that the book "The Greatest *Unsolved* Murder Mysteries" has disappeared. While Betty looks for it everywhere, Constable Flynn is lifting *fingerprints* off the *cash register* and the table it was sitting on. Perhaps the murderer has left his prints there. All other places – the bookshelves, the front door and the *scattered* books – are useless because the *fingerprints* of everyone in the village and lots of tourists must be on them as well.

"If we find prints on the *cash register* and over at Margaret's house that are not her own prints and that *match*, then we probably have the murderer's *fingerprints*," he thinks aloud.

"But then we still have to find the murderer who *match*es those prints," Betty responds logically.

He *nods*. "You're right, Betty. That's because you're a smart girl."

Betty's rosy cheeks turn a bit rosier. She wishes he would call her "Bette" once in a while. That's what almost everyone in Rosemeadows calls her because her last name is Davis. It is nice to be called by the name of that American actress. They even made a song about her, didn't they? "Bette Davis Eyes..."

Everybody calls her Bette Davis. Only Errol Flynn – well, Harold – does not.

But at least he thinks she's clever. That's a start, isn't it? So she says, "If the book is missing, that must mean there is some information about Ashley in it. Either Margie took it with her, and then we will find it at her house, or the murderer has taken it. But I know where to get a copy of the book."

Harold, who is *stroking* his Errol-Flynn-moustache and thinking hard, looks up in surprise. "Oh? Where is that? A large bookshop in London? I mean it could be *out of print*, couldn't it?"

"At Azamon," Bette explains. "That's the largest bookshop in the world. They sell old and new books through the Internet."

Übung 8: Lesen Sie weiter und setzen Sie die richtigen Präpositionen in die Lücken ein!
(without, at, of (2x), with, in, to)

ÜBUNG 8 !

"Really?" Harold is *impressed*. Her knowledge (1.) ______ computers and the Internet always surprises him. (2.) ______ him all that modern electronic stuff is a *closed book*. Secretly he wishes the world was still (3.) ______ computers, Internet, mobile phones and all those other ultramodern *gadgets*. But if you must live with it, it's good to have a secretary who knows how these things work.

Specially if it is a good-looking girl like young Bette (4.) ______ her rosy cheeks and *bright* eyes. Sometimes she's even got Bette-Davis-eyes – but you can't tell her that if you're her boss, can you? And anyway, better not give her the wrong idea.

He *sighs* and pulls the key to the bookshop out (5.) ____________ his pocket. "Let's lock up here and drive over to Margaret's house," he says more *gruffly* than he intended to sound.

He does not look (6.) ____________ her. If he did, he would see the happiness (7.) ____________ her smoky blue eyes.

Chapter 3: A Second Murder Mystery

Apparently the murderer had the same idea. When Flynn and Betty arrive at Margaret Prim's *cottage*, everything has been *turned upside down* – even the rose pots in the front garden.

"Why didn't I think of that earlier?" Flynn *sigh*s. "If Ashley didn't find what he was looking for in the bookshop, then his next stop had to be her house!"

"But why didn't he search the shop and *cottage* the night he *poisoned* her?" Betty wonders.

"Well, he probably didn't have time for that. Perhaps he was afraid of getting caught by one of her friends or neighbours."

Unfortunately, all the *fingerprints* Flynn *lifted* in the bookshop were those of Margaret Prim herself. Whoever broke into her shop and *turned* it *upside down* must have worn gloves. And he had no better luck with the *fingerprints* found inside her *cottage*. Of course most of them were her own prints, and the rest could be identified as well. They were all from people living in Rosemeadows. He even found two of his own *fingerprints* and a few that were Betty's.

"It would have been too easy," he says to his assistant back at the police station. "I am not having any luck with this *case*. What about you? Have you had any luck?"

"Yes, I have," Betty replies with a satisfied smile. "Even though Azamon didn't have the book, I did find another copy of 'The Greatest *Unsolved* Murder Mysteries'."

"Where did you find it?"

"Why, at Bebay, of course!" When she sees the *puzzled* look on his face she hurries to explain. "It's a sort of second-hand Internet shop. At Bebay you can get anything: slightly used clothes, brand new socks, television sets, antiques and even houses! They sell everything for a fixed price or in an auction to the person who offers the highest price."

"That's fascinating," Flynn replies dryly. "As long as you didn't make an offer for slightly used socks or an antique TV set."

"Of course I didn't. But perhaps you would like a dog? While I was surfing on the Internet, I also found the sweetest-looking, slightly used poodle, under two years old, that desperately needs a new home..."

Flynn shakes his head. "No. Definitely NOT. It's not that I don't like dogs, but how could I take care of him when I'm at work every day?"

"Take him with you to work every day," Betty answers quickly. "He could be our police mascot. We could name him Sergeant Poodle, couldn't we?"

Flynn turns round so that Betty can't see that he is smiling. He *grabs* the *fingerprint* report off his *desk* and puts it into the Prim *Case* File. Sergeant Poodle? A police mascot indeed! What a thought! Even though it WOULD be nice to have a dog around...

ÜBUNG 9

Übung 9: Formulieren Sie die Sätze in der Gegenwart!

1. Ashley didn't find what he was looking for in the bookshop.

2. Perhaps he was afraid of getting caught.

3. The murderer must have worn gloves.

4. Most of the fingerprints were her own.

5. Betty saw the sweetest-looking poodle.

6 . He could be our police mascot.

7 . It would be nice to have a dog.

But he does not say it. Better not give Betty any more ideas about getting him a dog. Otherwise she really will *adopt* that poodle. And anyhow, he would not know how to take care of a dog. A dog is something Harold Flynn has always dreamed about but never seriously *considered*.

Just like love. Too complicated. He tried it once and *failed*. But he is a quick learner. He will never make THAT mistake again. After

all, you live and learn, right? Compared to women and poodles, it is a *piece of cake* to look for a burglar or a car thief. Or even a murderer.
Flynn takes the *fingerprint* report off his *desk* and puts it into the Prim *Case* File. "So when will you have time to read the book?" he asks his assistant.
"As soon as I receive it in the post. Hopefully tomorrow. Then I can read it overnight. Will it be o.k. if I come in later on Friday? I mean, it's quite a thick book, and our *clue* about this Ashley may be in a later chapter."
IF we find a *clue* about Ashley in the book, that is, Flynn thinks to himself. Aloud he says, "If you need to, you can take Friday off. Just call me about your findings when you've finished your *research*."

Betty is busy. She is *working overtime*. And she loves her work – tonight more than ever. Just think: A real murder mystery! And there must be a *clue* in this book! And SHE is going to find it! Even if it takes her all night, she will find it.
She will find it, and Harold will be *impressed*. What did he say the other day? "That's because you're a smart girl."
Could that be a *declaration of love*? How did his voice sound when he said it? Was it *tender*? Soft? Or did it sound *gruff*?
All of the above would mean that he really likes her.
Only a neutral voice would mean that he does not care for her – apart from thinking she is a smart girl.
Betty is not only a smart girl but also an amateur psychologist. She knows enough about a man's psyche (and voice) to know that a rough or *gruff* or scratchy *male* voice can either mean a *sore throat* or be a sign of love. Usually the kind of love the man does not want to *admit* to himself. But better than a *sore throat*.

ÜBUNG 10 !

Übung 10: Lesen Sie weiter und unterstreichen Sie die jeweils richtige Verbform!

She *glances* at the alarm clock that (1.) ticks/is ticking by her bedside. It is 3:52 a.m. Then she (2.) takes/is taking another Belgian chocolate out of the box and (3.) *settles back*/is *settling back* into her pillow. While she (4.) *nibbles*/is *nibbling* on the Vanilla Cream praline, she (5) turns/is turning another page in the book and starts (6.) read/reading about the next *unsolved* murder mystery.

At noon Harold Flynn sits at his *desk* and *stares* out of the window. The thick *fog* outside makes him feel depressed – and sorry for himself. Or is it because Betty is not in today? Because her chair remains empty, her computer screen is a black hole, and her smoky blue eyes don't look at him today? Because he has to eat a lonely sandwich all by himself?

Nonsense, he *scolds* himself and takes a bite from his lonely chicken salad sandwich. The reason for feeling bad must be the fact that he is not getting any further in his *investigations* into the murder *case*. This is the first (and hopefully last) real murder *case* he has ever had. He must *solve* it. After all, that is the least he can do for Margie Prim.

While he is thinking, eating and making a chain out of paper clips, the phone rings.

"Hello, Chief!" He hears Betty's *cheerful* voice on picking up the *receiver*. "I've got good news and bad news. What would you like to hear first?"

"The good news," Flynn says while he is wondering what the bad news could be.

"I think I have found Ashley."

"You have?" Flynn asks *breathlessly*.

Betty can tell that he IS *impressed*. Good. That way he will *swallow* the "bad news" more easily.
"Well, an Ashley is *mentioned* in one of the *unsolved* murder *cases*. In a rather spectacular murder *case* that happened about twenty years ago. Back then, an actor named Sir Michael Blakely was found *poisoned* in his flat. He was playing Hamlet at the Royal Theatre at the time. After his death, his role was given to another actor – a *bloke* named Ashley St. John. That role made his career. But St. John was not a *suspect*. The police believed that Blakely's wife had something to do with the murder of her husband, because he had so many affairs with other women. But they could not link the crime to her. So the *case* was never *solved*."
Flynn is even more *impressed* with her findings. "That does sound like our *suspect*!" he says. "This Ashley St. John should be easy to find. What kind of *poison* was used to kill Sir Blakely?"
"Cyanide," Betty reports triumphantly.
Flynn whistles through his teeth. "That's interesting. Yes, Ashley St. John seems to be the man we are looking for," he says thoughtfully. "After all, there must be a reason why Margaret said 'It had to be Ashley' and why she was *poisoned*. Perhaps she *stumbled upon* something, but it must be more than just a story in a crime book."
"Perhaps he was looking for something else in the bookshop?" Betty wonders. "Apart from that book, I mean."
"Yes, there must be another *clue*. Margaret must have seen, heard or read something that made her so sure about Ashley, and so nervous that she couldn't tell Edith Pearson in the shop. Something that made Ashley murder her before she could tell another living soul about it."
"And we'll find out what that was," his assistant says *cheerfully*. "Don't you want to hear the bad news as well?"

Flynn is a bit afraid of hearing bad news coming from Betty. Is she planning on *quitting* her job? Perhaps she wants to marry one of the young *blokes* who keep asking her out?

No, he decides. He doesn't really want to hear her bad news. Not today. Today is Margaret Prim's *funeral*.

"Can't it wait until Monday?" he asks in a *gruff* voice. "I really don't want to hear any bad news today. Will you come to Margaret's *funeral* this afternoon?"

The *telephone line* goes quiet for a long moment. Flynn wonders if he has *offended* Betty without knowing it. But then she says, "Why, of course I will be there. I'll see you then."

Not only Betty, but the whole village of Rosemeadows *shows up* at Margaret Prim's *funeral*. Most people come because they liked Margie. Others come because nothing else ever happens at Rosemeadows. And some *show up* because of the food that is served at the Pearson's home after the *funeral*.

"I say, no one makes better *scones* than you do," says the farmer Willy Jones to the village baker, Robbie Benson, as he takes his third *scone* from a large *basket* that Benson brought in for the *gathering* after the *funeral*.

"But no one made better *lamb stew* than Margie Prim," replies Benson.

"But I heard it was *poisoned*," says Mary McCarthy, the local *hairdresser*. "That's what killed her – and her cat."

"Isn't it shocking?" Carmen Taylor shakes her pretty head. She is the waitress of 'The Black Rose', Rosemeadow's only restaurant, café and pub all in one.

"Yes, it IS shocking," says Flynn. He has joined the crowd that has *gathered* in front of the shortbread *basket*. That way he might hear something that could help his *investigation* AND get some of the delicious shortbread before it is all gone. He is also avoiding Betty and her bad news.

"I know you can't talk about the *investigation*, Errol, but do you have any *clue* who *poisoned* her?" Mary asks him.

Everyone looks at him.

"As you said, I can't talk about it," Flynn replies.

"Oh, that sounds mysterious!" Mary cries. "It sounds as if you DO have a *clue*! Is it somebody local?"

"That's all we need," Willy Jones says. "First a rainy summer and a bad *crop* – and now a murderer *in our midst*!"

Flynn regrets having said anything at all. "No, no," he says and shakes his head, "I didn't say it was someone from Rosemeadows."

"What about that *bloke* who had tea and *scones* at the 'Rose'?" Carmen Tailor asks. "That tourist who *showed up* the day Margie was *poisoned*?"

Flynn almost *chokes* on his shortbread. "What did you say? A tourist at 'The Black Rose' last Friday? I didn't know about any *strangers* in Rosemeadows! Why didn't you tell me? It might be important! Did he say anything to you? What did he look like?"

Carmen tries to remember. "Well, he was in his forties, I would say. Kind of a good-looking *chap* with a beard, but too old for me. He asked me why I was *wasting* my life in the middle of nowhere. Yes, that's what he said: 'In the middle of nowhere'. He said I could be a model with this pretty face and beautiful body."

"He was *hitting on* you," says the village baker. "That sounds like a murderer alright – some *stranger* who comes to our village and starts *hitting on* our local women!"

"And anyway, this is not the middle of nowhere," Farmer Jones adds. "We have the best farmland in the South of England."

"And the most beautiful women," says Harold Flynn. He is smiling at Carmen but thinking of Betty. "Well, what else did he say?"

Carmen smiles back at him. Then she remembers. "Oh yes – he asked about a *road map*. He said he was just passing through and wanted to know where he could buy a *road map*."
Flynn looks at her thoughtfully. "That's interesting," he says, but he cannot tell her why.
The *stranger* was looking for a bookshop in Rosemeadows. Or he was looking for its owner – Margaret Prim.

Chapter 4: A Trip to London

ÜBUNG 11

Übung 11: Lesen Sie weiter und setzen Sie ***the*** *oder* ***a*** *vor die Substantive!*

Betty has not said anything else about her bad news, and Flynn does not want to ask her. It is safer to talk about (1.) ________ murder *case*. So later in the car he says, "There must be something else that Margaret found out (2.) ________ day she was murdered. After all, the missing book was not (3.) ________ new book in her shop."
"But there were other new books," Betty responds quickly. "Remember (4.) ________ box that was *knocked over* in her shop?"
Flynn throws (5.) ________ *glance* at her. He should not have done that. She is looking at him with those smoky blue eyes. They make him lose his concentration. He quickly turns away and *stares* through (6.) ________ *windshield* of his car.
"Of course I remember. What about the box?"

"It's from (7.) ____________ shipping company up in London. I looked at the sender's address.

It was probably (8.) ____________ *consignment* of old or new books that arrived for Margie just before she died. She was very *neat*, you know. The box was still in the shop, so (9.) ____________ *consignment* must have arrived the same day or the day before."

Flynn *nods* slowly. "All those books that were *scattered* on the floor... You're right, they were probably new books she was putting away. And then she found something that made her say that thing about Ashley to her friend Edith."
"But the books near the box were not new," Betty points out. "They were all used books. Some of them had a name written on the inside of the *cover*."
Again Betty's sharp eye impresses Flynn. Sometimes she notices things even he misses. If she *quits* her job and marries one of the young local *chaps* like Tom Jenkins or Rick Fielding, it will be a great loss for the *police force*.
And not only for the *police force*...
"Do you remember what name?" he asks rather *gruffly*.
Betty is surprised by his *gruff* voice. She *glances* at him quickly, but his eyes are on the road. It is after Margaret Prim's *funeral*, and he is driving her home. "Let me see – what was it? O yes, I think it was Witherspoon. Mary Beth Witherspoon. A pretty name, I thought when I saw it."
Right now Harold Flynn does not care about pretty names. All he cares about is finding the person who killed Margaret Prim.
He doesn't even care about Betty's news – bad, good or otherwise.

See if he cares whether she leaves him to marry Tom Jenkins or Rick Fielding!

He stops his car in front of Betty's little white *cottage* with the blue door and window *frames*.

"Good work, Betty!" he says without looking at her. "Have a nice weekend. See you on Monday."

He steps on the gas pedal and *speeds off* rather fast for a police officer who knows the local speed limit. Betty *stares* after him and wonders what that was all about.

Overnight the weather turns, and Sunday is one of those few *bright* days in November when the sun smiles down from a clear blue sky. It is one of those Sundays when Constable Flynn has nothing better to do than think about a *case*. In fact, he has nothing to do at all. He pours himself the third cup of tea and *stares* out of the kitchen window. He keeps thinking about Margaret Prim and her secret. He thinks about this mysterious Ashley. He thinks about an Internet shop called Bebay where you can buy used books and even houses, and of course that reminds him of Betty. What is she doing today? Going to the cinema with Tom Jenkins? Or going for a walk with Rick Fielding – that dog!

His thoughts start wandering off to other types of dogs, to nice dogs, and suddenly he thinks how nice it would be to have a dog – a real dog. That thought surprises him.

He quickly shakes it off like a *bothersome flea*. What about all those other days? The *foggy* ones, the rainy ones, the busy days when he is *working overtime*?

No dog. Better think about that book *consignment* from London. What was the name again? A pretty name, as Betty said. Something Witherspoon. The name "Macbeth" keeps coming to mind, but he does not want to call up Betty (in case she is out on a date – or in with her date, which would be even worse). It can't be "Macbeth", that's not a name, not really...

Mary Beth. Of course. Mary Beth Witherspoon.

The phone company has a Mary Beth Witherspoon listed in Kensington. When he calls the number, it is answered after the third ring. It is the housekeeper, and she tells him that the lady of the house *passed away* three weeks ago. When he asks if he can stop by this afternoon for a few questions, she does not sound too *thrilled*.

"What is it with you *bloke*s from the *police force*?" she asks. "Do you have to *bother* people on Sundays now, too? Why are you never around when you're needed? Like the other night – I had to call the police because of a terribly loud party. They were making that horrible noise they call 'techno music', and the whole neighbourhood was shaking! It reminded me of World War II, when the German bombers were flying over London! And do you know how long I had to wait till the police finally *showed up*?"

"No, Madam, I don't know," Flynn replies *politely*. "But I'm sure you're going to tell me."

"Well, long enough to drink two cups of hot chocolate AND eat a ham-and-cheese sandwich AND watch a whole episode of '*Laurel and Hardy*'!"

Impatiently Flynn rolls his eyes but says *politely*, "You're right – that really IS quite a long time. Down here in Rosemeadows we usually respond within five minutes. But then we're a small village and London is a big city, isn't it?"

The housekeeper *agrees* and *calms down* enough to allow him to stop by in the afternoon.

"And it won't take a whole episode of '*Laurel and Hardy*' either, madam," he promises. Unless you talk as much in person as you talk on the phone, he thinks as he hangs up.

ÜBUNG 12

Übung 12: Lesen Sie weiter und tragen Sie die folgenden Adjektive in die Lücken ein!
(new, small, old, silver, rusty, sunny)

London on a Sunday is as busy as London on a weekday, and after two hours of driving through the (1.) ________________ countryside it takes Flynn another hour to get to Kensington. Half an hour later he finally finds the house he is looking for. It is a beautiful (2.) ________________ *mansion* in need of a (3.) ________________ *coat of paint*, some garden work and a few other repairs. It looks exactly like the kind of home where two ladies might live without money or *male* helpers.

A (4.) ________________ sign on the gate says BEWARE OF THE DOG, and when Flynn rings the (5.) ________________ doorbell, he hears a dog *yap*. It sounds like a (6.) ________________ dog, a poodle or terrier, not the kind of dog that would *scare* anyone *away*. They should add BUT PLEASE DON'T RING THE DOORBELL to the sign, he thinks with a smile.

A woman in her fifties opens the front door. A *yapping* white ball of *fur* with two shiny black eyes and a shiny black nose shoots out of the door and dances around Flynn's legs.
"Buster – get back inside the house! Come here, Buster, will you!" the woman calls out loud.

"That's a nice dog you have there," he says, and he even means it.
"Yes, he is. But unfortunately I must give him away. I can't stay here, so I am moving to a small flat where I am not allowed to keep a dog. Someone is coming to pick him up this afternoon. Buster, get back inside, will you?"

One hour, two cups of tea and three *scones* later Constable Flynn has learned from Lilly, the housekeeper, everything he needs to know. Yes, Lady Witherspoon does have a son named Ashley. He is a *successful* actor who calls himself Ashley St. John. However, he has not spoken to his mother or visited her for twenty years. Mrs Witherspoon never talked about him, and Lilly does not know the reason for that. But she remembers seeing the name Ashley in her lady's old *diary*. Of course she never read Lady Witherspoon's personal *diary*. But one day, while she was *dusting* the books on the *shelves*, it fell on the floor and opened at a page where her lady had written something about Ashley and his acting career. After Lady Witherspoon's death the *diary* was packed with the other books on the *shelves*, and the whole box was taken away by the company that is handling the *estate* sale.
"I wanted to give the *diary* to Ashley, but after his mother's death he called me and told me to sell all her books. So I forgot. And when he came over to decide what to do with the rest of her things, the box with the books was already gone. He got very *upset* about that and said that, after all, the *diary* was the only personal thing he was *inheriting* from his mother," Lilly reports. "But the *strange* thing is that when I said I would call the company that picked up the books, he did not want me to do that. He shook his head and said I shouldn't *bother*."
That's interesting, Flynn thinks, but he cannot tell the housekeeper that. So instead he just says, "Hmm... Well, thank you very much

for your time and the delicious *scones*. I must be going back now, before it gets too *foggy*."

The housekeeper looks disappointed. She is quite enjoying the company of the police officer (who reminds her of that famous American actor – what was his name again? Ah yes, Errol Flynn!).

"Oh really? If you like, you can stay for supper," she says.

But Harold Flynn shakes his head and gets up. He is reaching for his jacket when the doorbell rings. Buster starts *yapping* again.

"Oh, that must be the young woman who is coming over to pick up Buster," Lilly says. When she looks at the dog, her face suddenly turns sad. "I'm going to miss you, little doggy. I hope you have a happy new home."

"Well, I'll be leaving now," Flynn says and opens the front door.

But he is not leaving after all.

The young woman with the rosy cheeks and the smoky blue eyes standing outside on the doorstep is Betty Davis.

ÜBUNG 13 !

Übung 13: Lesen Sie weiter und setzen Sie das passende Satzzeichen ein!

Of course Flynn would not let his assistant take the train back to Rosemeadows (1.) ___ While he is driving back south, Betty explains everything to him. Buster is sitting on her lap (2.) ___ enjoying the attention his new mistress is paying him.

"You see, nobody wanted to take poor Buster. So I had to *adopt* him! It's as simple as that. Since you don't want a dog (3.) ___ I decided to keep him myself."

(4.) ___ And where will you keep him while you're at work (5.) ___" Flynn wants to know.

"I (6.) ___ ll take him with me to the office, if that is alright with you."

"And what if it is NOT alright with me (7.) ___"

"Then I'll *quit* my job," Betty replies. "From now on you get a package deal: Buster and me – or *neither of us*."
Flynn thinks about that for a second. "Well, then I'll have to take the package deal, won't I?" he says. "After all, I wouldn't know what to do without my new police mascot..."
Betty just looks at him with those smoky blue eyes and smiles. Harold almost runs his car off the road.
After about five minutes he finally dares to ask, "What about that bad news you wanted to tell me the other day?"
"Bad news? What bad news?" Then she remembers. "Oh, yes! This is it – the bad news is that I am the new *proud* owner of a slightly used poodle named Buster! Why, what did YOU think?"
"I thought the bad news was some other dog," Flynn replies quickly.
"What other dog?" Betty does not understand what he means.
"Like Tom Jenkins or Rick Fielding," he says *gruffly* and wonders why she suddenly starts laughing.
Then she pays even more attention to the dog and does not look at Flynn until they are back in Rosemeadows, and he wishes he were a dog named Buster.

When Flynn and Betty go inside the bookshop once again to look for Mary Beth Witherspoon's *diary*, it is not among the books.
"So that is what the murderer was looking for when he broke in

here," Flynn finally says. "That's exactly what I thought."
"Me, too," Betty says. "The question is: DID he find it? Did he find it here or at her *cottage*?"
"That's what we will have to find out now. Let's go over to her house and have a look."
Betty calls Buster, who is *sniffing* at the books on the floor and ignoring her. "Look", she says, "he's *wagging his tail*. That's because he likes me."
Flynn *glances* at the dog. "No, he's *sniffing* at a mystery. That means he likes murder *cases*. Come over here, B. N. Buster!"
The little dog runs over happily to the police officer, *wagging his fuzzy tail*.
"B. N. Buster?" Betty asks.
"Bad News Buster," Flynn explains. "That's his official title. He's the new mascot of the Rosemeadows one-man-one-woman police force – and he is bad news for criminals! Aren't you, Buster?"
Buster's answer is a *determined* yap.

While Harold Flynn is searching the whole *cottage* for the missing *diary*, Betty steps out into the garden. The last few days have been cold. Sadly she looks at the frozen rose *blossoms* and thinks of Margaret.
Buster runs over to the far end of the garden. He starts *sniffing* at one of the rosebushes in the corner. Then he looks at her and *wags his tail*.
"What is it, Buster?" she asks. "Do you like roses, too?"
But when she comes nearer to the bushes and takes a closer look at the spot, she is surprised. The *soil* around that one rosebush looks freshly *turned over*. That's *strange*. It means that the flower was planted only a few weeks ago. But why? After all it is November – a bit late in the year for planting rose bushes.

She quickly walks over to the back door. “Errol – I mean Harold!” she calls. “Take a look at this!”
A few moments later Flynn comes outside. Betty points at the rose-bush. “This bush is newly planted. Look at the *soil*. You usually don’t plant flowers in November.”
Harold *nods* slowly. Then he starts to dig out the *soil* and finally pulls out the freshly planted rosebush. He is not all surprised when a plastic bag appears beneath the plant.
Betty watches *breathlessly* as he pulls the plastic bag out of the *soil*.
Inside they find a small book bound in leather. It has a broken *brass lock*, and it is Lady Witherspoon’s *diary*.

Übung 14: Lesen Sie weiter und unterstreichen Sie jeweils das passende Wort!

ÜBUNG 14 !

The next day Flynn comes in early. (1.) *Impatiently/Impatient* he waits until Betty comes (2.) about/in with the new police mascot. Of (3.) certainly/course it is *mainly* the dog he is *looking forward to*, as he tells (4.) himself/him. But for some unknown reason he (5.) felt/feels nervous when the young (6.) woman/women walks into the station at two minutes after eight. There really is no logical reason (7.) for/to being nervous.

After all, they have got Ashley. It was all right there in Mrs Witherspoon’s *diary* – everything she knew about the murder. And she really did know everything. He murdered the other actor twenty years ago only to get the role of Hamlet. He built his career on a murder! And then, when Lilly told him about his mother’s *diary*, he became *worried* that someone might read it, and read about the murder of twenty years before. He called the company that delivered her books to find out where the books had gone. Then he drove out to Rosemeadows and went to the bookshop. He stood in front of the window and looked inside. That's when he saw Margaret Prim nervously whisper something to her friend Edith and point to a book next to the *cash register*. At that point he was sure that she knew about the *diary* and about the murder. So he had to kill her, too.

Late last night the London Police Force picked him up at his flat and took him to Headquarters for *interrogation*. He *confessed* to both murders. *Case solved*. So why is Flynn suddenly so nervous?
"It might be sunny next Sunday," he says as Betty hangs up her coat. She turns round without saying anything. She is not exactly making this easy for him.
"Well, I mean, IF it is sunny next Sunday", he tries again, "then I might want to take B.N. Buster out for a walk. If you don't *mind*, that is – I mean, if you have a date with Jenkins or some other *chap* it might be useful if I take the dog for a walk..."
He feels like a fool. Her eyes do that to him all the time. "Of course you can also come along, Bette – I mean Betty – if you don't have anything better to do, that is... And if it's not *foggy* next Sunday..."
His head feels *foggy*, and he thinks it is better not to say anything else about dogs and walks.
But she does not seem to think that. "No, I don't have anything better to do next Sunday," she says with a smile. "And I would love a walk in the *fog* with you, Harold."
Buster is *wagging his tail*, which means he *agrees*.

Abschlusstest

Übung 1: Übersetzen Sie folgende Sätze ins Englische!

1. Er kennt schon die Antwort.

2. Er tauscht die Gewehre aus.

3. Er will das Geständnis nicht sehen.

4. Er versuchte, mich zu erpressen.

5. Watson gratuliert sich.

6. Sie tun mir nicht leid.

Übung 2: Unterstreichen Sie das richtige Wort!

1. They quickly across/cross the street and stop the two strangers.
2. Bob is telling me all about/over his work.
3. I expect you're/your glad when the night is over.
4. My brother is a/an dentist.
5. Then he tells them/they the rest of the story.
6. All's well that ends good/well.

Übung 3: Bilden Sie negative Sätze!

1. They shoot ducks.

....

2. He's drinking a beer.

....

3. She wants to leave her husband.

....

4. Jobs may be lost.

....

5. Let sleeping dogs lie!

....

Übung 4: Welche Wörter gehören zusammen? Ordnen Sie zu!

1. to give	☐ the booty
2. to retrieve	☐ hand
3. to celebrate	☐ sale
4. a brass	☐ a pep talk
5. on the other	☐ band
6. to leave	☐ at a wine bar
7. to clear away	☐ advice
8. to shrug	☐ cups and saucers
9. a jumble	☐ someone in charge
10. to give	☐ one's shoulders

Übung 5: Welches Wort ist das „schwarze Schaf“? Unterstreichen Sie!

1. jacket, shirt, cloth, garment, trousers
2. restaurant, pub, tearoom, hothouse, coffee shop
3. sneeze, glance, nod, mumble, melt
4. lemon meringue, honeymoon, apple turnover, cream puff, tart
5. tall, large, pale, small, little
6. good, great, fine, well, pretty
7. why, where, while, when, who

Übung 6: Bilden Sie Fragen, die sich mit den folgenden Sätzen beantworten lassen!

1. Scott and Debbie went to Madame Tussaud's Wax Museum.

Where ....?

2. They found a note in John Lennon's shirt pocket.

What ....?

3. They went back to Madame Tussaud's to take a picture.

Why ....?

4. They were dressed in dark clothes.

How ....?

5. The secret meeting was at midnight.

When ....?

6. The woollen garment belonged to the blond woman.

Who ....?

Übung 7: Welche der folgenden Aussagen zur Geschichte „Learning by Killing“ sind wahr? Markieren Sie mit richtig ✔ oder falsch – !

1. Eastcastle is a small town in the North of England. ☐
2. Colonel Lessons wants to retire to Brighton. ☐
3. Tracy Dean was born in Ireland. ☐
4. Jim Ryan is a Catholic from Dublin. ☐
5. Mrs Bradley is a cleaner at the school. ☐
6. Elke comes from Switzerland. ☐

Übung 8: Welche Begriffe gehören zusammen? Ordnen Sie zu!

1. dog	☐ mansion
2. city	☐ sigh
3. murderer	☐ foggy
4. cottage	☐ cat
5. sunny	☐ village
6. laugh	☐ victim

Übung 9: Kreuzen Sie den jeweils korrekten Satz an!

1. a) ☐ Ted looks at her and gets up from his chair.
   b) ☐ Ted looks at her and got up from his chair.
   c) ☐ Ted looked at her and get up from his chair.

2. a) ☐ What book she was pointing at?
   b) ☐ What book pointed she at?
   c) ☐ What book was she pointing at?

3. a) ☐ The good doctor also gets invited to a lot of suppers.
   b) ☐ The good doctor gets also invited to a lot of suppers.
   c) ☐ The good doctor gets invited to also a lot of suppers.

4. a) ☐ Flynn wishes he is a dog named Buster.
   b) ☐ Flynn wishes he would be a dog named Buster.
   c) ☐ Flynn wishes he was a dog named Buster.

Übung 10: Formulieren Sie die Sätze im Passiv!

1. The housekeeper ate a ham sandwich.

....

2. Ashley poisoned the widow with cyanide.

....

3. Betty will pick up the dog on Sunday.

....

4. Did they find the murderer?

....

5. Edith is cradling the cushion.

....

6. Flynn drives Betty home.

....

Lösungen

It Was Murder, My Lord

Übung 1: 1. today/yesterday 2. to find/to lose 3. accurate/false 4. to begin/to finish 5. huge/small 6. wealthy/poor 7. wife/husband
Übung 2: 1. awful 2. table 3. gamekeeper 4. motorway 5. stranger 6. wine bar 7. weekend
Übung 3: 1. He 2. She 3. I 4. We 5. We 6. me 7. we 8. He 9. She 10. he 11. them
Übung 4: 1. to go back/with someone 2. to give/someone a lift 3. to flash/a smile 4. to arrive/at the house 5. to be interested/in a person 6. to sip/a drink 7. to sit/around a table 8. to smoke/a cigar 9. to invest/money
Übung 5: 1. banker 2. member 3. fork 4. friend 5. shout 6. mobile 7. shoulder
Übung 6: 1. He feels uncomfortable with the young Londoner. 2. The inspector shifts around in his chair. 3. The affair has nothing to do with him. 4. We have already got your written statement. 5. Bellforth is rather a pain in the neck. 6. There is a knock at the door. 7. He appears to be very worried.
Übung 7: 1. bring 2. goes 3. gives 4. are 5. calls 6. are 7. like 8. got 9. ends up
Übung 8: 1. falsch 2. richtig 3. richtig 4. richtig 5. falsch 6. falsch 7. richtig
Übung 9: 1. happen 2. are 3. sign 4. accept 5. has 6. gets 7. takes 8. is
Übung 10: 1. to calm down/to relax 2. napkin/serviette 3. to brush aside/to ignore 4. to understand/to comprehend 5. melody/tune 6. arrangements/plans 7. urgent/important 8. road/street 9. problem/trouble
Übung 11: 1. am playing 2. walks 3. know 4. sees 5. am having 6. gives 7. is leaving
Übung 12: 1. Er muss eine Aussage bei der Polizei machen. 2. Natürlich können Sie sich an den Rest erinnern. 3. Bellforth spricht mit einer aggressiven Stimme. 4. Fisk hat einige Informationen. 5. Plötzlich beschließt er zu gehen. 6. Sie können sich absolut auf mich verlassen. 7. Er öffnet die Tür zum Wohnzimmer.
Übung 13: 1. At eight o'clock the next morning Macey is in the office. 2. You need a head beater for a successful shoot. 3. Gordon is arriving this afternoon. 4. Macey and Sally sit down and talk in the kitchen. 5. Macey gives Sally a crinkled handkerchief when she begins to cry. 6. Rodney does not want to throw away his stamp collection. 7. When Macey visits Sally Hardcastle the sun is shining.

Midnight in the Park

Übung 1: 1. have 2. tries 3. ordered 4. eat 5. did 6. be 7. is cutting
Übung 2: 1. why 2. what 3. what 4. what 5. what 6. why
Übung 3: 1. from 2. round 3. in 4. of 5. for 6. for 7. of 8. from
Übung 4: 1. restaurant 2. dinner 3. curries 4. midnight 5. park 6. dark 7. park bench 8. feet 9. moon

Übung 5: 1. coming 2. shines 3. holding 4. taking 5. hear 6. start 7. tries 8. could
Übung 6: 1. wide = breit 2. young = jung 3. tall = hoch/groß 4. dead = tot 5. sudden = plötzlich 6. soft = weich 7. tender = zärtlich
Übung 7: 1. A baby is in the bundle. 2. Debbie stumbles over a dead tree branch. 3. The woman left a jacket/woollen garment behind. 4. Debbie finds three matchboxes. 5. The name and address of a pub are printed on the matchboxes. 6. Debbie notices that the jacket smells of smoke.
Übung 8: 1. But 2. Sorry 3. nothing 4. way 5. middle 6. too 7. Good
Übung 9: 1. a 2. the 3. a 4. the 5. a 6. the 7. the
Übung 10: 1. on 2. about 3. of 4. at 5. of 6. for 7. in 8. to 9. to
Übung 11: 1. Die Kartenspieler wollen zahlen und gehen. 2. Wir müssen ihr ein großes Trinkgeld geben. 3. Es sah so aus, als wäre die Kellnerin misstrauisch geworden. 4. Wie wäre es, wenn ich das/dieses Bier austrinke? 5. So wird niemand Verdacht schöpfen. 6. Scott verzieht das Gesicht und verlässt hastig den Tisch.
Übung 12: 1. fine 2. full 3. into 4. broke 5. everything 6. from 7. couldn't

Learning by Killing
Übung 1: 1. laugh/cry 2. plump/slim 3. whisper/shout 4. cheap/expensive 5. late/early 6. short/tall 7. superb/terrible 8. heavy/light 9. fast/slow
Übung 2: 1. ugly 2. car 3. garden 4. arrive 5. clever 6. secretary 7. huge 8. seagull 9. receipt 10. sailor
Übung 3: 1. smile 2. laugh 3. looks 4. come 5. means 6. know 7. think 8. can 9. produce 10. depends 11. have
Übung 4: 1. magazine 2. desk 3. biro 4. briefcase 5. folder 6. chips 7. redhead 8. class
Übung 5: 1. is 2. am talking 3. am trying 4. means 5. nods 6. says
Übung 6: 1. You can put logs on a fire. 2. Karl picks up his biro. 3. The Swiss Franc is cold and antiseptic. 4. People meet their friends in a pub. 5. She decides that Karl must die. 6. You are an innocent witness. 7. Jim is happy that the ice is broken.
Übung 7: 1. falsch 2. falsch 3. falsch 4. richtig 5. falsch 6. falsch 7. richtig
Übung 8: 1. by 2. about 3. over 4. at 5. out 6. off 7. off
Übung 9: 1. cocky/impertinent 2. cut/commission 3. issue/distribute 4. under false pretences/illegally 5. calm/relaxed 6. grand/thousand 7. vigorously/energetically
Übung 10: 1. think 2. leaves 3. rushes 4. hurries 5. follows 6. is lying 7. is dying
Übung 11: 1. Sie sind bereit, ihre Aufgaben zu präsentieren. 2. Die Studenten lachen und plaudern miteinander. 3. Sie freuen sich auf die Aufführung. 4. Mahdi verschwindet hinter den/dem Vorhang. 5. Ich fahre weg und dann schießt du. 6. Karl putzt seine Brille. 7. Einige Studenten fangen an zu schreien.
Übung 12: 1. was 2. were 3. understood 4. left 5. knew 6. heard 7. thought
Übung 13: 1. Ryan's class can give no useful information because they are upset. 2. The toy gun cost £5.50. 3. Olsen's seat was in the second row. 4. Olsen

heard three sounds. 5. Tracy was at home on Friday. 6. The cleaner's name is Mrs Bradley. 7. Olsen lives in Denmark.
Übung 14: 1. Is Watson doing his interviews? 2. Do they order another gin? 3. Does he turn to the gun collection? 4. Does he laugh hysterically? 5. Does his school pay local taxes? 6. Is she cleaning the floor? 7. Is the sun setting on Eastcastle?

Murder in Rosemeadows
Übung 1: 1. insisted 2. was acting 3. sighed 4. could not believe 5. forgot 6. said
Übung 2: 1. moments 2. room 3. garden 4. blossoms 5. wallpaper 6. flowers 7. sofa 8. ground 9. glasses
Übung 3: 1. measles 2. a headache 3. a broken arm 4. a toothache 5. the flu 6. seasickness
Übung 4: 1. walks 2. look at 3. wake up 4. talked 5. think 6. calling 7. presses 8. going 9. looking for 10. take
Übung 5: 1. juice 2. window 3. supper 4. widow 5. jams 6. soothe 7. feel 8. shine 9. driveway
Übung 6: 1. at 2. from 3. in 4. after 5. of 6. about
Übung 7: 1. Show me your window. 2. Flynn swallows the lump in his throat. 3. He turns the shop key in the lock. 4. The name is written on the front window. 5. We may have our murderer. 6. Let's go over to her shop.
Übung 8: 1. of 2. To 3. without 4. with 5. of 6. at 7. in
Übung 9: 1. Ashley doesn't find what he is looking for in the bookshop. 2. Perhaps he is afraid of getting caught. 3. The murderer must wear gloves. 4. Most of the fingerprints are her own. 5. Betty sees the sweetest-looking poodle. 6. He can be our police mascot. 7. It will be nice to have a dog.
Übung 10: 1. is ticking 2. takes 3. settles back 4. is nibbling 5. turns 6. reading
Übung 11: 1. the 2. the 3. a 4. the 5. a 6. the 7. a 8. a 9. the
Übung 12: 1. sunny 2. old 3. new 4. rusty 5. silver 6. small
Übung 13: 1. . 2. , 3. , 4. " 5. ? 6. ' 7. ?
Übung 14: 1. Impatiently 2. in 3. course 4. himself 5. feels 6. woman 7. for

Lösungen Abschlusstest

Übung 1: 1. He already knows the answer. 2. He exchanges the guns. 3. He does not want to see the confession. 4. He tried to blackmail me. 5. Watson congratulates himself. 6. I do not feel sorry for you.
Übung 2: 1. cross 2. about 3. you're 4. a 5. them 6. well
Übung 3: 1. They do not shoot ducks. 2. He is not drinking a beer. 3. She does not want to leave her husband. 4. Jobs may not be lost. 5. Do not let sleeping dogs lie!
Übung 4: 1. to give/advice 2. to retrieve/the booty 3. to celebrate/at a wine bar

4. a brass/band 5. on the other/hand 6. to leave/someone in charge 7. to clear away/cups and saucers 8. to shrug/one's shoulders 9. a jumble/sale 10. to give/a pep talk

Übung 5: 1. cloth 2. hothouse 3. melt 4. honeymoon 5. pale 6. well 7. while

Übung 6: 1. Where did Scott and Debbie go? 2. What did they find in John Lennon's shirt pocket? 3. Why did they go back to Madame Tussaud's? 4. How were they dressed? 5. When was the secret meeting? 6. Who did the woollen garment belong to?

Übung 7: 1. falsch 2. falsch 3. falsch 4. falsch 5. richtig 6. richtig

Übung 8: 1. dog/cat 2. city/village 3. murderer/victim 4. cottage/mansion 5. sunny/foggy 6. laugh/sigh

Übung 9: 1. a 2. c 3. a 4. c

Übung 10: 1. A ham sandwich was eaten by the housekeeper. 2. The widow was poisoned with cyanide by Ashley. 3. The dog will be picked up by Betty on Sunday. 4. Was the murderer found (by them)? 5. The cushion is being cradled by Edith. 6. Betty is driven home by Flynn.

Glossar

AE	amerikanisches Englisch
fam	umgangssprachlich
fig	bildlich
pl	Plural
v	Verb

accommodation	Unterkunft
account	(Bank-)Konto
accounts *pl*	Geschäftsbücher
accuse *v*	beschuldigen
adjourn *v*	vertagen
admiringly	bewundernd
admit *v*	zugeben
adopt *v*	adoptieren; sich zulegen
afford *v*	sich leisten
agree *v*	zustimmen
alert	wach
alley	Gasse
allowance	hier: Beihilfe, Zulage
almond	Mandel
apple turnover	Apfeltasche
appreciation	Anerkennung
arsonist	Brandstifter(in)
at stake	auf dem Spiel
attentively	aufmerksam
awkwardly	ungeschickt
backfire *v*	hier: fehlzünden, nach hinten losgehen; fehlschlagen
bad luck	Pech
baffled	verwirrt, verdutzt
bangers and mash *fam*	Würstchen mit Kartoffelbrei
bargain	günstiges Angebot
barrel	Gewehrlauf; Fass
basket	Korb
beam *v*	strahlen
bear, bore, born *v*	hier: ertragen; tragen

beater	Treiber(in)
bedsit	Einzimmerwohnung
be *v* **hard on someone**	hier: stressen, schlauchen *fam*
be *v* **mistaken**	sich irren
bend	Kurve, Biegung
be *v* **overcome by a sudden fit of laughter**	einen plötzlichen Lachanfall bekommen
bet, bet, bet *v*	wetten
betrayal	Verrat
betrayed	betrogen; verraten
biro	Kugelschreiber
blackmail	Erpressung
blackmail *v*	erpressen
blank	hier: verständnislos; leer, unbeschrieben
blink *v*	blinzeln
bloke *fam*	Kerl *fam*, Typ *fam*
blood pressure	Blutdruck
blossom	Blüte
blossom *v*	blühen
booty	Beute
borrow *v*	ausleihen
bosom	Brust
bother *v*	sich die Mühe machen; belästigen
bothersome	lästig
bow *v*	verbeugen
branch	Ast, Zweig
brass band	Blaskapelle
brass lock	Messingschloss
break (broke, broken) *v* **the ice** *fig*	das Eis brechen *fig*
breathlessly	atemlos, außer Atem
briefcase	Aktentasche
bright	intelligent; hell; strahlend
brush *v*	hier: streifen; bürsten
brush *v* **aside**	abtun, verwerfen
buddy *fam, AE*	Kumpel *fam*
by the way	übrigens
calm *v* **down**	sich beruhigen
canary	Kanarienvogel

canvas	Leinwand
cartridge	Patrone
case	Fall
cash register	Kasse
catch (caught, caught) *v* **up with**	einholen
cautiously	vorsichtig
centre *v* **around**	sich drehen um
chap *fam*	Kerl *fam,* Bursche *fam*
cheerful	fröhlich, heiter
chestnut tree	Kastanienbaum
choke *v*	sich an etwas verschlucken; ersticken; (er)würgen
chuckle *v*	kichern, in sich hineinlachen
circumstances *pl*	Umstände
claim *v*	hier: vorgeben, angeben; einklagen
cling (clung, clung) *v* **to**	haften an, sich klammern an
closed book *fig*	Buch mit sieben Siegeln *fig*
cloth	Stoff; Tuch
cloud	Wolke
clue	Hinweis, Indiz
coat of paint	Farbanstrich
cocky *fam*	großspurig, frech
coincidence	Zufall
commercial break	Fernseh-/Radiowerbung
companion	Begleiter(in)
complain *v*	klagen, sich beschweren
complexion	Teint
composed	beherrscht, gelassen
confess *v*	gestehen
confession	Geständnis
confusing	verwirrend
con-man *fam*	Schwindler
conscience	Gewissen
consider *v*	überlegen
consignment	Lieferung, Sendung
convince *v*	überzeugen
convincing	überzeugend
cope *v* **with**	mit etwas fertig werden

copper *fam*	Polizist(in), Bulle *fam*
coroner's court	Gericht für unnatürliche Todesfälle
corpse	Leiche
cosy	gemütlich
cottage	kleines Landhaus
counter	Bartheke
cover	Tarnung; Titelseite; Einband
cradle *v*	in den Armen wiegen
cream puff	Windbeutel, Sahnetörtchen
crinkled	zerknittert
crook *fam*	Gauner(in)
crop	Ernte
cuff *v* **someone round the ear** *fig*	jemandem eine Ohrfeige geben
curse *v*	hier: fluchen; verhexen
cushion	(Sofa-)Kissen
cut	hier: Anteil, Provision; Schnitt
death-blow	Todesstoß
deceased	Verstorbene(r)
declaration (of love)	(Liebes-)Erklärung
deep-dish pizza	in einer Schüssel gebackene Pizza mit dicker Kruste
deliberate	absichtlich, vorsätzlich
dentist	Zahnarzt, Zahnärztin
depend *v* **on**	abhängen von
desk	Schreibtisch
desperate	verzweifelt
determined	(fest) entschlossen
dial tone	Wählton
diary	hier: Tagebuch; (Termin-)Kalender
die *v* **of (un)natural causes** *pl*	eines (un)natürlichen Todes sterben
distract *v*	ablenken
divorce	Scheidung
doorknob	Türklinge, Türgriff
dress rehearsal	Generalprobe
drive(way)	Auffahrt zu einem Haus
drowsy	schläfrig
duke	Herzog
dull	langweilig, eintönig

dust *v*	abstauben
earl	Graf
eavesdropper	Lauscher(in)
embarrassed	verlegen
embrace	Umarmung
emergency	Notfall
encouraging	ermutigend
envelop *v*	einhüllen
error	Fehler
estate	Landgut, Anwesen; Nachlass
every cloud has a silver lining *fig*	jedes Unglück hat auch sein Gutes
evidence	Beweis(e)
exchange *v*	wechseln, austauschen
exploit *v*	ausbeuten; nutzen
fail *v*	scheitern, versagen
familiar (with)	bekannt, vertraut; sich auskennen (mit)
Fancy that! *fam*	Stell dir vor!
farewell	Abschied (nehmen)
fate	Schicksal
faulty	fehlerhaft
fee	hier: Schulgeld; Gebühr
feel (felt, felt) *v* **(ill) at ease**	sich (un)behaglich/(un)wohl fühlen
fellow *fam*	Kerl *fam*, Bursche *fam*
fidget *v*	herumzappeln
figure	Gestalt; Figur; Zahl
fingerprint	Fingerabdruck
fire precautions	Brandschutzmaßnahmen
fireproof	feuerfest
fishy *fam*	hier: verdächtig, zweifelhaft, faul *fig*
flabbergasted	vollkommen verblüfft
flash	Blitz(licht)
flattered	geschmeichelt
flea	Floh
fog	Nebel
foggy	neblig
fold *v* **up**	zu Grunde gehen; zusammenfalten
frame	Rahmen
frantic	völlig verzweifelt

freshen *v* **up**	sich frisch machen
frown *v*	die Stirn runzeln
funeral	Beerdigung
fur	Fell
fuss *v* **around**	Aufhebens machen, ein Theater machen
fuzzy	wuschelig, kraus
gadget	Gerät
gamekeeper	Wildhüter(in)
gaping	klaffend
garment	Kleidungsstück
gather *v*	(sich) versammeln; zusammenbringen
gathering	Versammlung, Zusammenkunft
get (got, got) *v* **it off your chest** *fig*	etwas loswerden; sich etwas von der Seele reden
giggle *v*	kichern
give (gave, given) *v* **someone a lift**	jemanden (im Auto) mitnehmen
glance *v*	(flüchtig) blicken, einen Blick werfen
glasses *pl*	Brille; Gläser
Gone With The Wind	Vom Winde verweht
go (went, gone) *v* **off**	hier: losgehen
goods *pl*	Waren, Güter
grab *v*	an sich reißen, ergreifen, zupacken
grand *fam*	tausend Pfund; großartig
gratitude	Dankbarkeit
grimace *v*	das Gesicht verziehen, eine Grimasse machen
growl *v*	knurren, brummen
grown	hier: erwachsen; gewachsen
gruff	mürrisch
guardian	Wächter(in)
gulp	(großer) Schluck
gunsmith	Büchsenmacher(in)
hairdresser	Friseur(in)
hand *v* **in one's notice**	kündigen
handcuffs *pl*	Handschellen
handkerchief	Taschentuch
handsome	gutaussehend
hardly	kaum

hash browns *pl, AE*	Bratkartoffeln
hearty	herzlich, herzhaft
heave *v* **a sigh of relief**	erleichtert seufzen
hedge	Hecke
heir	Erbe, Erbin
hesitate *v*	zögern
hip flask	Flachmann
hit man *fam*	Killer
hit (hit, hit) *v* **on** *fam*	anmachen, anbaggern *fam*
honeymoon	Flitterwochen
hothouse	Treibhaus, Gewächshaus
illuminated	beleuchtet
impatient	ungeduldig
impertinence	Frechheit, Dreistigkeit
impostor	Betrüger(in)
impressed	beeindruckt
in charge (of)	verantwortlich (für); die Aufsicht haben
in our midst	mitten unter uns
in the final analysis	im Endeffekt
incident	Zwischenfall, Ereignis
inherit *v*	erben
inheritance	Erbe, Erbschaft
innocent	unschuldig; ahnungslos
inquest	gerichtliche Untersuchung der Todesursache
interrogation	Verhör
investigation	Ermittlung, Untersuchung
invisible	unsichtbar
invitation	Einladung
involved	verwickelt, involviert
issue *v*	herausgeben, verteilen
jealous	eifersüchtig
jingle	hier: Klingelton
jumble sale	Flohmarkt; Wohltätigkeitsbasar
keep (kept, kept) *v* **an eye on** *fig*	im Auge behalten
knock *v* **over**	umwerfen, umstoßen
know (knew, known) *v* **the ropes** *fig*	sich auskennen

lamb stew	Lammeintopf
landlord	Vermieter; Gast-, Kneipenwirt
Laurel and Hardy	Dick und Doof
lawn	Rasen
lawyer	Rechtsanwalt, Rechtsanwältin
Let's call it a day. *fig*	Lasst uns Schluss machen (für heute).
let (let, let) *v* **sleeping dogs lie** *fig*	schlafende Hunde nicht wecken *fig*
library	Bibliothek
lie (lay, lain) *v* **ahead**	bevorstehen; vor jemandem liegen
lift *v* **fingerprints**	auf Fingerabdrücke untersuchen
loll *v*	leblos fallen
look *v* **forward to**	sich freuen auf
loom *v* **on the horizon** *fig*	drohend am Horizont heraufziehen *fig*, sich bedrohlich abzeichnen
loopy *fam*	verrückt, bekloppt *fam*
loosen *v* **one's collar**	den Kragen lockern
lump	Klumpen
mainly	hauptsächlich
make (made, made) *v* **a clean breast of it** *fig*	alles gestehen
male	männlich
manor	Landsitz, Herrenhaus
mansion	herrschaftliches Wohnhaus, Villa
marksman	Scharfschütze
match	Streichholz
match *v*	übereinstimmen; (zusammen)passen
matchbox	Streichholzschachtel
measles	Masern
mellowed brickwork	alter Ziegelsteinbau
melt *v*	(ver)schmelzen
mention *v*	erwähnen
message	Nachricht, Botschaft
mind *v*	hier: jemandem etwas ausmachen, etwas dagegen haben
mist	Nebel
mix-up	hier: Verwechslung; Durcheinander
mix *v* **up with**	hier: verwechseln
mock	hier: gespielt; falsch

modestly	bescheiden, anständig, züchtig
money for old rope *fig*	leicht verdientes Geld
moonlighting *fam*	Schwarzarbeit
mop *v*	wischen
muddled up	durcheinander
mumble *v*	murmeln
napkin	Serviette
neat	hier: ordentlich; sauber
neither of us	keine(r) von uns beiden
nibble *v*	knabbern
night shift	Nachtschicht
nod *v*	nicken
note	Notiz; kurze Mitteilung, Zettel; Banknote
novel	Roman
objective	Ziel
obviously	offensichtlich
occasion	Gelegenheit
offend *v*	kränken, beleidigen
orphan	Waise
out of print	vergriffen (Buch)
outcome	Resultat
outhouse	Nebengebäude
over the moon *fig*	überglücklich, von etwas hin und weg sein
overhear, overheard, overheard *v*	zufällig mithören
pain in the neck *fam*	Nervensäge
pale	blass, bleich
pancake with maple syrup	Pfannkuchen mit Ahornsirup
park bench	Parkbank
pass *v* **away**	sterben
patrol car	Streifenwagen
patroness	Mäzenin
pavement	Bürgersteig, Gehsteig
pebble	Kieselstein
pep talk *fam*	aufmunternde Worte, Motivationsgespräch

piece of cake *fig*	ein Kinderspiel *fig*
pile	Haufen, Stapel
plump	pummelig, mollig
poacher	Wilderer
poaching	Wildern, Wilderei
poison	Gift
poison *v*	vergiften
police force	Polizei
polite	höflich
pond	Teich
pot roast	Schmorbraten
pottery	Keramik
pounce *v* **on**	sich auf etwas stürzen, über etwas herfallen
pray *v*	beten
preserve *v*	erhalten, in Stand halten; konservieren, einmachen (Obst, Gemüse)
pretend *v*	so tun als ob, vortäuschen
promotion	Beförderung
pronounce *v* **a judgment**	ein Urteil abgeben
pronounce *v* **dead**	für tot erklären
property	hier: Immobilie, Landbesitz; Eigentum
props *pl*	Requisiten
proud	stolz
pull *v* **up**	im Auto anhalten
Punch and Judy show	Kasperletheater
put (put, put) *v* **two and two together** *fig*	zwei und zwei zusammenzählen *fig*, den Durchblick bekommen
puzzled	verwundert, verständnislos
queasy	übel, schlecht
question *v*	befragen
quid *fam*	Pfund (Geld)
quit, quit, quit *v*	hier: kündigen; aufgeben
rape	Vergewaltigung
receipt	Quittung
receiver	Hörer (Telefon)
recipe	Kochrezept
recognize *v*	wieder erkennen
refurbished	restauriert

regret *v*	bereuen, bedauern
reliable	zuverlässig
rely *v* **on**	sich verlassen auf
remote control	Fernbedienung
replacement	hier: Ersatzperson
research	Recherche, Forschung
responsibility	Verantwortung
rest *v* **in peace**	in Frieden ruhen
retrieve *v*	apportieren (Jagdhund); zurückholen
rev *v* **up**	den Motor aufheulen lassen
reveal *v*	enthüllen, aufdecken
road map	Landkarte
roar *v* **off** *fam*	abdüsen *fam*
run, ran, run *v*	hier: leiten
sack race	Sackhüpfen
scare *v* **away**	verscheuchen, wegjagen
scattered	verstreut
scold	(aus)schimpfen
scone	Teebrötchen
scramble *v*	stürzen, hasten; klettern
send *v* **daggers** *fig*	tödliche Blicke zuwerfen *fig*
setting	Schauplatz
settle *v* **back**	sich zurücklehnen
shadow	Schatten
shelf, shelves *pl*	Regal, Regale
shelve *v* **the case**	den Fall zu den Akten legen
shepherd's pie	Hackfleisch und Kartoffelbrei
shift *v* **around**	sich hin und her bewegen
shiver *v*	zittern
show *v* **up** *fam*	auftauchen, erscheinen
shrug *v*	die Achseln zucken
shuffle *v*	hier: schlurfen
shyly	schüchtern
sigh *v*	seufzen
sip *v*	nippen
skeleton in the cupboard *fig*	Leiche im Keller *fig*
slam *v*	zuschlagen, zuknallen
sleeve	Ärmel
slump *v*	sich fallen lassen

smirk *v*	süffisant lächeln, selbstgefällig grinsen
smoothen *v* **out**	glätten
smuggle *v*	schmuggeln
snap *v*	hier: zerbrechen; (zu)schnappen
sneak *v*	schleichen
sneeze *v*	niesen
sniff *v*	schnüffeln, schnuppern
snoop *v, fam*	herumschnüffeln
soil	Erde
solve *v*	lösen
soothe *v*	beruhigen, lindern
sore throat	Halsschmerzen
sparkle *v*	funkeln
speck	Körnchen; Pünktchen
speed (sped, sped) *v* **off**	davonrasen
splutter *v*	spucken (beim Sprechen); stottern, stammeln
staff	Kollegium; Personal
stamp	Stempel; Briefmarke
stare *v*	starren
starve *v* **(to death)**	(ver)hungern
stately home	herrschaftliches Anwesen
statement	Aussage
stay	Aufenthalt
steward	Verwalter(in)
Stock Exchange	Börse
straighten *v* **out**	zurechtrücken
strange	merkwürdig, seltsam
stranger	Fremde(r)
strawberry tart	Erdbeertörtchen
stream	Bach
stroke *v*	streiche(l)n
stuff *v*	stopfen
stumble *v* **(over)**	stolpern (über)
stumble *v* **upon**	zufällig auf etwas stoßen
stunned	benommen; fassungslos
success	Erfolg
successful	erfolgreich
suggest *v*	vorschlagen; andeuten

sum *v* **up**	zusammenfassen
Sure did! *fam*	Klar doch! Logisch!
surrounded by	umgeben von
survive *v*	überleben
suspect	Verdächtige(r)
suspect *v*	verdächtigen
suspicious	misstrauisch; verdächtig
swallow *v*	(herunter)schlucken
sweat *v*	schwitzen
take (took, taken) *v* **a back seat** *fig*	weniger Verantwortung übernehmen; in den Hintergrund treten
take (took, taken) *v* **off**	ausziehen; abheben, abfliegen
tall order *fig*	schwierige Aufgabe
tearoom	Teehaus, Teestube
telephone booth	Telefonzelle
telephone directory	Telefonbuch
telephone line	Telefonleitung
tender	zärtlich
thrilled	begeistert, hingerissen
throat	Kehle
thud	dumpfes Geräusch
tick *v* **off**	abhaken
tickle *v* **someone's fancy** *fig*	jemanden reizen
tie *v*	binden
ties *pl*	Bindungen
tiff *fam*	Geplänkel, kleiner Streit
tip	Trinkgeld
toad-in-the-hole	in Teig gebackene Würstchen
tomcat	Kater
tormented	gequält
traffic jam	Verkehrsstau
tranquillity	Stille
treasure chest	Schatzkiste, Schatztruhe
trembling	zitternd
Trooping the Colour	Feier zum Geburtstag der Königin
turn *v* **over**	übergeben; umdrehen
turn *v* **upside down**	auf den Kopf stellen
twinkle	Zwinkern
twist *v* **someone's arm** *fig*	hier: jemanden überreden

under false pretences	unter Vorspiegelung falscher Tatsachen
undertaker	Leichenbestatter(in)
unsolved	ungelöst
upkeep	Erhaltung
upset	bestürzt, verstört
urgent	sehr wichtig, dringend
venison	Wildfleisch
vigorously	energisch, kräftig, heftig
vividly	hier: lebhaft; lebendig
volume	hier: Band, Buch
wag *v* **one's tail**	mit dem Schwanz wedeln
waste *v*	verschwenden
watch *v* **closely**	aufmerksam beobachten
wax museum	Wachsfigurenkabinett
wealthy	wohlhabend, reich
well *v* **up**	hochsteigen (Tränen)
What's up? *fam*	Wie geht's?
white as a sheet *fig*	kreidebleich
widow	Witwe
wig	Perücke
wind farm	Wind(energie)park
windowsill	Fenstersims
windshield	Windschutzscheibe
witness	Zeuge, Zeugin
witty	geistreich, witzig
work *v* **overtime**	Überstunden machen
worried	besorgt, beunruhigt
worse for wear	fertig *fam*, betrunken; abgenutzt
wrapped up	eingewickelt
wrinkle	(Gesichts-)Falte
wrist	Handgelenk
yap *v*	kläffen
yard	ca. 91cm (Maß); (Innen-)Hof
Yellow Pages	Gelbe Seiten